P9-ASF-969

Speech and Theater

THE LIBRARY OF EDUCATION

A Project of The Center for Applied Research in Education, Inc.

G. R. Gottschalk, Director

Categories of Coverage

I	II	III
Curriculum and Teaching	Administration, Organization, and Finance	Psychology

IV	V	VI
History, Philosophy, and Social Foundations	Professional Skills	Educational Institutions

Speech and Theater

THORREL B. FEST

*Professor and Chairman,
Department of Speech and Drama
University of Colorado*

MARTIN T. COBIN

*Associate Professor of Speech and Drama,
Departmental Coordinator of Graduate Studies
University of Colorado*

The Center for Applied Research in Education, Inc.
Washington, D.C.

Foreword

Brain power is the greatest asset in the world today. This fact accounts for the present urgent scrutiny of education.

Experts are examining their various fields in an effort to make contributions to the development of the full intellectual potential of every living human being. Surveys of research give evidence that many laws and customs of the past are no longer applicable, and substitutions and adaptations must be made to fulfill present-day needs.

Among the areas most vital to the broad program of education is that of oral communication through which society has evolved and man has developed. Dr. Fest and Dr. Cobin in *Speech and Theater* accept the responsibility for establishing that socialization carried on through speech should be the central concern of students, teachers, administrators, and laymen. They recognize the complexity of the behavior of man as he produces effective talk for the purpose of controlling society. They have gathered and examined both early and recent descriptive, historical, experimental, and quantitative research and have included in this volume what they consider significant and pertinent. They have shown that the roots of the area are in the classical tradition but that the branches have grown and spread and now reflect changes in culture and times.

These authors introduce speech and theater as part of the whole field of education related to every discipline in the curriculum; but, as practical and honest educators, they do not claim that oral communication alone makes the effective individual; they do, however, insist that successful living is impossible without it.

Readers will find this the most enlightening book on speech and theater which has been published in a long time. In direct, simple, clear, and precise language, Fest and Cobin show the importance of their area in the maximum use of brain power for free democratic living and, indeed, for the survival of the human race.

GLADYS L. BORCHERS

Professor Emeritus,
Education and Speech
University of Wisconsin

Contents

CHAPTER I

The Nature of Speech

The Concept of Communication

Human beings are continuously engaged in a process of adapting to their environment. To achieve a satisfactory adaptation, men must understand the environment and they must be capable of making meaningful responses to it. Explorations designed to increase understanding are, in essence, meaningful responses. Other meaningful responses are found in attempts to control the environment, attempts to profit from what it has to offer, and attempts to minimize the harm it can do. Communication contributes greatly to man's ability to understand and to respond.

Communication can function on a variety of levels. The Stone Age savage rolling boulders down a hill at a stranger approaching his cave exemplifies an elementary level of communication. A more advanced level is exemplified by the craftsman who engages in repetitive demonstrations to communicate the intricacies of a relatively complex process—such as weaving. As the complexity of the information to be communicated increases, as the distance in time and space through which the communication is to carry increases, and as the number of people to be involved in the communication increases, there is a corresponding rise in the level of communication. That is, the communication itself becomes more complex until it requires the development of a language capable of dealing with actuality in abstract or symbolic terms.

(Language employs symbols in certain standardized patterns of interrelationship. The symbols stand for actualities—specific objects or concepts. The user of a language must understand both the symbols and the patterns. "The angry boy kicked the horse" is meaningless to anyone who does not understand such symbols as "angry," "kicked," and "horse." But knowledge of the symbols is not, in and of itself, sufficient to distinguish between the information carried by "the angry boy kicked the horse" and "the horse kicked the

1

angry boy." Any student of a foreign language knows the value of a good dictionary and also the fact that a good dictionary does not guarantee a correct or even a meaningful translation.

The complexities of language are not deficiencies but, rather, the very elements that enable language to meet the needs of advanced-level communication. Language enables men to deal in abstractions. Abstractions permit communication in the absence of the elements symbolized. Abstractions also permit involved manipulation. Each of these tremendous advantages can be exemplified in very simple terms. A person need not have a pencil in order to get one. He can talk about what he wants. He can even order a pencil made to specifications such that it will be different from any pencil previously made. This exemplifies the value of communication in the absence of the symbolized elements. In addition, a person can ask for three pencils for each member of a particular group. Whoever seeks to respond to this request need only respond to the abstraction of individual existence. That is, there is no need to consider the personalities, occupations, origins, beliefs, or any of a host of other dimensions pertaining to the members of the group. From the complexity of what each individual is, there is abstracted the single item of individual existence. One individual existence is added to another until the total is determined. Considering only the abstracted quality of "number" is to consider very little. What is known about a group, really, when all that has been determined is the number of individuals it includes? Obviously, not much, but nonetheless all that is necessary to achieve the desired manipulation of a number that can be multiplied by three to determine the quantity of pencils to be obtained. This, then, illustrates the value of abstracting elements that can be manipulated.

The Nature of Speech

All languages are alike in that they employ symbols and standardized patterns of symbol interrelationship. Languages differ from one another, however, to the extent that each particular language employs its own set of symbols and its own standardized patterns. The speaker of English employs a different set of symbols and patterns from the speaker of Japanese; these speakers employ different languages.

The speaker of English may address an audience in a face-to-face situation while his speech is at the same time carried to many others by means of radio. This can be described as an example of a speaker employing one language to communicate by means of two different media. It must be recognized, however, that the change in medium influences the use of language. Radio will distort the pitch range of the speaker and, possibly, alter the way in which the speaker utilizes sudden and drastic changes in volume level. Radio, obviously, eliminates the visual reinforcement of the speaker. This, in turn, may result in an actual distortion of the communication. Consider, for example, a speaker who asks a series of three rhetorical questions. He may follow the first two questions with a "thumbs down" gesture and a facial expression of complete rejection. He may follow the third question with a "thumbs up" gesture and a smile of smug contentment. The radio listener might be aware of nothing more than a pause at the end of each question. In addition to such factors as these, radio may influence the speaker by making him conscious of the much wider audience available to him. He may respond to this broader audience by choosing vocabulary that is not quite so precise as he could use in addressing the particular audience before him but that is less likely to be beyond the reach of many who might "tune him in" on their home receivers. In fact, the speaker may be so motivated to adapt to his radio audience that his "live" audience becomes quite conscious of this adaptation. Instead of radio listeners feeling that they are provided the opportunity to hear an address by a specific speaker to a specific audience in a specific place, the situation may be one in which a "live" audience gathers together feeling that it has the opportunity to watch a specific speaker give an address to a radio audience.

The modifications of language resulting from changes in the medium of communication may become so great as to suggest that the original language has been abandoned in favor of another language. The primary language that men developed for high-level communication involving symbolizations and manipulative abstractions was a language of speech. Written language constituted a great advance for mankind, for it extended the communicative use of language and freed it of dependence on memory. Written language must be recognized, however, as growing out of an attempt to record the spoken language. The written and the spoken media are

different. The modifications resulting from changing back and forth
between the medium of writing and the medium of speech are
extensive. Whether or not one accepts the degree of change as sufficiently extensive to result in language change, the reality of modification and of change must be recognized.

Failure to recognize the nature of the relationships and differences between writing and speaking is widespread. It is exemplified
by the tendency to think of the vowels as the written letter symbols
a, e, i, o, and *u.* The pronunciation rule regarding the definite ar-
ticle *the,* which is to be pronounced differently depending on
whether it is followed by a vowel or a consonant, is clear enough
when "the man" is contrasted with "the egg"; it is a bit confusing
to some people when the contrast is between "the only egg" and
"the one egg." When such confusion exists, it arises from the tendency to think of "one" and "only" as written symbols, both of which
start with the vowel *o,* rather than as speech symbols starting with
entirely different sounds. This failure to recognize relationships and
differences has serious consequences. It results in a belief that skill
in writing and skill in speech are interchangeable, that training in
one will be the equivalent of training in the other, that the effective
writer would be a good choice for a person to speak before an audience, and that extensive training in written language with little
or no formal training in spoken language will equip a person to
function in a society in which most of the communicative activity
is oral.

Speech has been defined in a variety of ways. Central to the academic discipline that concerns itself with this subject as its primary
focus is the process by which men adapt their own bodies as linguistic vehicles to serve their communicative needs in exploring,
controlling, and adjusting to the environment in which they exist.
The process in itself is complex. The applications of the process
are varied. Working within the academic discipline of speech, therefore, are people with a great diversity of areas of specialization. As
specializations, these areas often give the superficial impression of
being somewhat unrelated. Their interrelationships can be explored
theoretically or within the framework of historical development.

The Existence of a Tradition

Theories concerning the origin of speech are necessarily hypothetical. Certain facts are clear, however. Men adapted, for speech, physiological organs that served other and more basic functions. The existence of speech as a secondary or overlaid function is apparent in the fact that the speech function must always wait until the physiological function is performed whenever there is a conflict between the two. Men developed language while they developed speech. Speech functions as a language; it involves a speaker and a listener who have a common understanding of acoustic symbols and accompanying visual symbols—all of which are produced by the human organism of the speaker in standardized patterns of interrelationship and are received by the listener who is capable of hearing the sounds, seeing the gestures, and arriving at a meaningful interpretation of the information being conveyed.

Although frequent reference has been made to communication as a conveying of information, there is a need to understand the fact that nothing tangible actually travels from one person to another. The speaker does not *give* anything to the listener; he *excites, stirs up, stimulates*. What the speaker succeeds in stimulating is not completely under his control but is, in large part, dependent on the listener and everything in the past experience of the listener that conditions his understanding and his interpretation—that is, his response—as he reacts to the stimulus. The possibility of differences in understanding and interpretation is inherent in the fact that speech, as a language, employs symbols and abstractions that lend themselves to extensive manipulation. The ability to communicate about elements not present is, in itself, a significant manipulative act; but the manipulative potentialities are far more complex than this. The potentialities include the intimate relationship between speech and thought. In developing manipulative abstractions for communication, man also developed manipulative abstractions for thinking. Thought need not always employ the manipulative abstractions of speech; however, a great deal of it does.

What emerges from any serious consideration of the nature of speech is not only an awareness of its significance as language and as thought, but a respect for the skill necessary to employ it in effective communication and a sensitivity to the immensity of the task undertaken by anyone who would study it in any comprehensive sense. It is to be expected that the significance of speech, the need to employ it, and the difficulties encountered in employing it effectively in performing complex communicative tasks would lead men, at an early period of history, to give speech serious consideration and to study it systematically. Such was, in fact, the case. Evidence of this is to be found in the writings of Ptah Hotep in Ancient Egypt and in Corax's treatise on persuasive speaking written in Ancient Greece. The writings of Plato and Aristotle in Greece and of Cicero and Quintillian in Rome yield additional and readily available evidence of the attention which the men of antiquity gave to the theoretical aspects of the subject.

From the time of antiquity up to and including our own generation, there has been a sustained tradition of speech theory. Classical theoreticians focused on rhetoric, the art of persuasion. The conduct of affairs in those days was oral to such a degree that no distinction was made between the persuasion accomplished through speech and the persuasion accomplished through writing. The persuasive use of language was the concern of the rhetoricians. Many modern rhetoricians still focus on this concern, embracing within their scope the language of writing as well as the language of speech. Other modern rhetoricians consider their particular area of focus to be the persuasive use of the language of speech. With either view, however, the rhetorician deals with a subject of vital concern to democratic societies. It is significant that this phase of the speech discipline has flourished most in those societies in which there has been a high development of democratic social institutions. This is not to suggest that persuasive speech is limited to democratic societies. In other societies, the persuasive situation differs and the skills required for persuasion differ; persuasive speaking, nevertheless, exists. The chief difference, however, is that persuasion through speech is not considered as integral and necessary a part of the formulation and the expediting of decisions in a nondemocratic society as it is in one that is democratic. As a consequence, the development of the rhetorical skill of the citizenry as a basic contribution to the effectiveness with which society can function is necessary only to democracies.

Speech is employed, of course, for many purposes other than those associated with the institutions of government or of formal, organizational decision-making. Speech is used, as well, for the give-and-take of social interaction and for clearly artistic purposes. These uses of speech have also been the subject of careful study ever since the days of antiquity. Aristotle's *Poetics* has played at least as significant a role as his *Rhetoric*.

Although the impact of the classical theoreticians and practitioners has been felt throughout the subsequent development of the speech discipline, there have been other major contributions. Among these have been contributions growing out of a variety of emphases: on speech delivery, on the physiological speech process, on the psychology of speech, on the role of speech in group processes, and on the interrelationship of speech with other media of communication. The historical development is far too extensive and complex to be treated here. Excellent sources exist. A cursory treatment of the subject runs so great a risk of creating tremendous distortion through oversimplification that it is best avoided entirely. What is pertinent and capable of being stated succinctly is the fact that the modern student of speech, whatever his area of specialization, is the inheritor of a long and continuous tradition.

The diversity of the modern speech field is most clearly manifested by a listing of the areas claiming the greatest number of specialists. Such a listing would include rhetoric, public speaking, interpretation, theater, debate, discussion, radio-television, speech education, speech science, speech and hearing rehabilitation, and speech in organizational communication. Whatever else each area demands of whoever would specialize in it, each and every one includes a concern with and a knowledge of the use of speech to communicate. Moreover, the concern would not be limited to the mechanics of how this is accomplished; it would extend to questions of motivation and of ethical responsibility.

The Physical Basis

Air passes back and forth between the lungs and the atmosphere by means of the trachea, or windpipe, that connects the lungs to the throat cavity. A valve at the top of the trachea can seal off this passageway. This device is useful to prevent foreign matter from entering the lungs or to impound air within the lungs so that the chest cavity will serve as a solid base for the muscular action of the arms.

The valve itself is composed of two structures of muscle, cartilage, and connective tissue. Each of these structures is capable of covering half the diameter of the trachea. Viewed from above, these structures appear to be two flat strips of muscle with relatively thin, bright edges forming a floor across the trachea with a slit through the middle—from front to back—where they approximate each other. Viewed from below, they appear to be two arched muscles, relatively thick at the side attachments to the trachea and curving upward to a thin edge as they approach each other. The edges of these structures, at the point where they can contact each other, are the portions of the valve generally referred to as the *vocal folds* because of their secondary function in speech. When the folds are brought together and held firmly, the valve is closed. The folds are always together at the front of the valve-housing cartilage system, but the back portions can be separated to open the valve and allow free passage of air. It is possible to bring the folds close to each other and then, by forcing the air between them, to set into vibration the thin edges of the folds. This action creates a tone. It is also possible to bring the vocal folds into a partially closed position such that the edges will not be set into vibration as air is pushed upward between them but so that there will be friction noises created by the air having to force its way through the narrow opening. This action creates the whispered sound normally associated with the alphabetical letter symbol *h*. In this case, the friction results in air vibrations although the vocal folds themselves are not vibrating. Changes in the air passages between the vocal folds and the outer air can modify the nature of the vibrations imposed on the outer air. This is true of tones created by vibrating vocal folds, sounds created by friction noises at the vocal folds, and friction noises created above the vocal folds. This last type of sound is exemplified by the action often associated with the letter symbol *th*, as in the word *thin*. In this case, the vocal folds are separated to allow air to come out from the lungs with no friction involved until the air is forced through a narrow opening between the tongue and the front teeth.

Wherever and however the air is forced into vibration, it vibrates back and forth through a certain distance, or amplitude, and at a certain speed, or frequency of vibrations per unit of time. The amplitude and frequency, within certain limitations, are interpreted by the listener as loudness and pitch, respectively. This interpretation is based on the action of the listener's eardrum, which is set into vibration by the vibrations of the outer air. The eardrum vibrations keep step with the air vibrations stimulated by the speaker, responding to changes in amplitude and frequency. This occurs, of course, to the eardrum of the speaker as well, allowing the speaker to monitor his own speech. The combined effect of amplitude and frequency is interpreted by the listener as intensity.

The vibrations of the vocal folds are complex rather than simple. That is, the over-all vibration of each fold is accompanied by faster vibrations of various segments. In addition to the presence of a dominant frequency, therefore, a number of other frequencies are present. As the dominant frequency changes, the entire complex changes and there are many changes in segmental vibrations. Some of the great variety of vibrations present, as well as harmonics of many of them, will be reinforced by the vibration of columns of air within the resonating cavities of the throat, mouth, and nose. This resonating reinforcement contributes to giving the voice an individual characteristic that the listener interprets as a quality of pleasantness or unpleasantness. Also contributing to this characteristic is the megaphone effect of the resonating cavities, an effect that is dependent on the size and shape of the cavities and their openings and on the tension, relaxation, and condition of the cavity walls. This dimension—quality—is what differentiates two voices producing sounds of the same pitch and loudness level. Change in quality is what makes a person sound different when he has a cold.

Speech is dependent, for its symbolic function, on the ability of the speaker to produce not only audible sounds but specific sounds and sound combinations that are sufficiently stable to be recognizable and usable in a language code. This is accomplished by the movement of the articulators: the lips, teeth, tongue, jaw, and velum. The velum is a valve of membranous tissue located at the throat end of the mouth and capable of being swung so as to direct the outward flow of air through the mouth, through the nose, or through both together in varying proportions. Speech is given a nasal quality to the extent that air is directed through the nose. Certain sounds used in English speech are formed precisely as nasal sounds, that is by blocking off the oral cavity at the lips, gum ridge, or velum. The three specific sounds just mentioned can be given

very loose label designations in the written symbols *m, n,* and *ng.*
Similar designations can be given to each of the other sounds employed in speech.

The use of written alphabet letter symbols as labels for speech
sounds lacks precision. Evidence of this is the inability of such a
system of labels to make the necessary distinctions between the *ng*
sounds of *hanger, angry,* and *singe,* the *gh* sounds of *ghost, tough,*
and *through,* or the *a* sounds of *ago, able, axe,* and *all,* to mention
only a few examples. The diacritical marks employed by dictionaries
were devised to cope with this need for a system of written symbols
to represent speech sounds. The most precise system devised for
meeting this need, however, is that of the *International Phonetic
Alphabet.* This system includes symbols for each sound in English
speech as well as for many sounds not employed in English speech
but serving as integral components of other language codes. Unlike
the other systems, phonetic symbolization provides one symbol—
and one only—for each speech element symbolized.

The sounds of speech are merely part of a language code. As
such, they must be clearly recognizable and they must be correct.
The speaker must employ the proper symbols and produce them
with sufficient clarity to avoid any confusion as to their identity.
Choice of the correct sound symbols is a matter of pronunciation.
Clarity of presentation is a matter of enunciation. Both are important if speech is to serve its communicative function. To serve this
function, however, it is not necessary for various repetitions of a
sound to be precisely alike; the need is for sufficient similarity to
allow no confusion as to what sound is intended and no diver-
sion of attention to the unusual manner in which the sound was
formed. In actuality, therefore, the phonetic symbols do not represent specific *sounds* so much as *sound families* or what are known
as *phonemes.*

The rate dimension of speech can be explained in a variety of
ways. Changes in the rapidity of movement of the articulators will
affect rate. The extent to which individual sounds are prolonged
will affect rate. Pause is also a factor in determining rate. Speech is
not merely a succession of phonemes. The phonemes are combined
into word symbols that, in turn, are presented within the framework of some particular linguistic pattern. The symbols are made
clear to the listener by correct pronunciation and precise enuncia-

tion. The pattern is made clear by the grouping of symbols and the interrelating of one group to another. This is accomplished by a variety of factors, including pitch inflection and rate. A major device in establishing such interrelationships is the use of pause. The placement of the pause and the duration of the pause affect the rate of speech and are an integral part of the patterning of speech. Rate tends to be inversely related to complexity of idea and of sentence structure, directly related to clarity of language and of enunciation.

The physical basis of speech can be summarized by reference to the effective use of voice and articulation. The voice should be loud enough to be heard easily and without discomfort to the listener. The pitch range should be great enough to allow for variety of expressiveness. The pitch should fluctuate around a particular level that exploits the reinforcing characteristics of the resonation system. Variations in pitch should reflect the purposes of the communication and should not labor under a superimposed and monotonous repetitive pattern. The voice should be pleasant. Pronunciation should be correct. Enunciation should be clear. The rate should reflect vitality and interest and a sensitivity to the communicative purpose. The rate should not be so rapid as to confuse the listener. Variations in loudness for purposes of relative emphasis, pitch inflections, and control of rate, including pause, should clarify for the listener the linguistic patterns being employed.

The speaker also works with a visual speech code. Usually, the visual dimension is an accompaniment, a vivification. At times, the visible actions of the speaker are more definitive. Whatever use the speaker makes of posture, facial expression, gesture, or changes in muscular tensions of the body, he must be aware that he speaks to a viewer as well as to a listener and that the entire communicative act is to be an integrated entity free of distractions that will weaken the communicative impact.

The Psychological Basis

The speaker seeks a response from one or more individuals who react to the stimuli created by the speaker. Mention has been made already of the fact that the speaker cannot control this response with any exactness. This suggests that meaning is not inherent in the speech itself. For the speaker there is a meaning. For the listener there is another meaning. Speech is the speaker's attempt to stir up in his audience, of one person or many, meanings that will approximate his own. In attempting to do this, the speaker is helped tremendously if the speaking situation is one that allows feedback, that is, the opportunity for the speaker to sense and adapt to the reactions of the listener. In such a situation, the speaker will respond to the responses and adapt his speech to the needs that become apparent in the very process of communicating. This process is facilitated when a speaker minimizes distractions and focuses audience attention on the communicative impact of the speech.

In developing an interplay between speaker and audience, there is need for considerable sensitivity on the part of the speaker. This is one aspect of what the speaker brings to bear on the situation. There are other factors as well, such as the speaker's health and vitality, his knowledge and motivation, and his attitude and sense of ethical responsibility. In the focus on the physical process of speech, care must be taken to maintain a constant awareness of the basic fact that speech communication is a human activity involving human interrelationships among human beings who exist as distinct individuals.

In regard to the human dimension, note should be taken of the fact that people react to environmental influences. Not only is a speech communication act conditioned by the individuality of the speaker and the distinct individualities of the various members of his audience; it is also conditioned by the speaking situation or occasion. The fact that the audience is large and that its members are interacting with one another may be an element in the situation. The fact that the audience has gathered for a particular purpose or with an awarenes of a common problem may be a part of the situation. The fact that the speaker is engaged in direct address, in a radio broadcast, in an interpretative reading of a literary work, in the creation of a dramatic character within a theatrical production, or in an intimate conversation affects the speaking situation. Clearly, then, the speaker employs a language code that interrelates two or more individuals in a particular communicative act within a specific communicative situation.

CHAPTER II

The Speech Cycle

The Reciprocal Relationship

Speaking and listening are reciprocal activities. The speaker is engaged in a basic form of self-expression. His message serves as a stimulus to those who hear and see him. Most frequently the speaker's purpose is to secure a response from the listener, the nature of which may depend on the attention given by the receiver and on the receiver's previous conditioning to all of the complex factors involved in a particular communicative situation. The speaker also stimulates himself. For the listener-receiver to respond effectively, he must have sensory adequacy, interest that goes beyond the most elementary attention, some capacity for interpretation of the message, and both a willingness and a capacity to change relationships. In short, the listener and the speaker, the receiver and the sender, are continually exchanging roles. This response and exchange may often be limited to sub-vocal speech, to varying degrees of bodily response, or to the recording in written form of information and ideas.

The listener-receiver's response will be limited by his intelligence, his skill as a receiver, and his background and experience. Assuming that his interest and motivation are such that he is willing to play the role of receiver, he must then understand how to behave in a given situation. This involves accepting and interpreting both oral and visual messages, as well as integrating the two appropriately. As his ability and experience assist him in giving meaning to these messages, he must then determine *how* to respond and *when* to respond.

At the same time, the speaker-sender is engaging in a parallel and related form of behavior. In addition to hearing himself, and, in some special circumstances, also seeing himself, he may observe the effects of his communication and use his observations as a guide to his continuing communicative behavior. His success depends not only on the same principles and forces that apply to the listener; additional factors are his own self-perceptions in the speaking role. Thus it becomes clear that, in this communicative relationship, two or more parties are engaged in a circular kind of process in which meaningful response is the principal objective. The relationship is flexible. The roles are reversible. Maximum effectiveness can result only from understanding of and skill in the several parts of the process. It is a highly complex, learned response that requires conscious and continuous effort if understanding is to be approximated and the process is to be improved. Success in communication tends to facilitate communication. Difficulties and failures tend to restrict communication.

Adjustive Speech

Speech as a form of self-expression is also a basic means by which man achieves adjustment. The drive of one human organism to adapt to other human organisms is universal in normal individuals. Coming into the world as a helpless infant and passing through a long period of childhood dependence and training, man depends upon adjustment for personal survival. As a social creature, too, man has attained his present position by such adjustment. From the most primitive to the most complex societies, his progress has paralleled his capacity to organize and work with others. By discipline and cooperation, he has been able to control his environment or adapt to it. In his more sophisticated relationships, man adjusts so as to preserve those things which he has valued highly. A major portion of this adjustment is psychological. Most people wish to establish pleasant reciprocal relationships with their fellow men. In short, we want to be liked by and, in turn, to like other people. Often these contacts are purely pleasurable, as seen in our casual conversations and social interactions with friends or neighbors. This need may be satisfied when we strike up a conversation with strangers, when we express a distaste for living in sparsely populated areas, or when we spontaneously express pleasure at seeing human habitation even though no physical need such as that for food, shelter, or medical attention exists. In many cases, contact with those who are dominant or hostile is preferred to isolation. The child may prefer unfavorable attention to being ignored; solitary confinement is considered one of the most severe punishments to which an individual may be subjected.

As the human organism constantly strives for adjustment, oral communication is one of the fundamental methods employed. Certainly it is one of the most convenient, swift, appealing, and effective means available. Each person can use it at his own discretion, and the results are often immediately evident. It is uniquely human, making possible a wide range of expression involving both facts and feelings. At the same time, it is flexible, allowing for a continuous adaptation to the most fluid part of the person's environment—the other people. When oral communication cannot be carried on conveniently and with a reasonable degree of accuracy, adjustment and development may be restricted for both the individual and the group. Witness the problems faced by persons suffering physical handicaps that interfere with their expression or reception of oral messages. Consider the extent to which language barriers sometimes isolate persons or groups more effectively than distance, geography, or culture. Sometimes special methods or means for interpersonal communication unite one group of individuals and exclude others. This is seen in the special language that young children may develop among themselves, in the vocabulary or jargon of specialists in a particular area, and in the continuous effort to add visual stimuli when seeking to communicate with those who speak a different language.

The individual's speech will reflect and be influenced by his adjustment as he moves through different levels of maturation and sophistication. As the individual progresses from infancy to adulthood, his needs and his perceptions will change. In turn his communication, if free and spontaneous, will reflect his changing ideas and feelings. Both the substance and the manner of the child's communication will differ significantly from that of the sophisticate. At the same time, the substance and form of communication directed to the individual as he develops will affect in some degree his maturation and sophistication. Clearly, communication by itself can be expected to have little, if any, effect on physical development; however, intellectual and social maturity may be influenced significantly by communication experience and skill. Much of what the individual receives, whether child or adult, comes to him orally. His response to this—in fact, his opportunity to communicate, to express, to inquire, to test, to be challenged, to succeed, and to fail—is essential if receptivity and flexibility are to develop. Thus, the potential for communication will affect the total personality.

From the foregoing, it is clear that the nature of man and his relation to his environment make his adjustment a dynamic process. Man has developed society and it in turn has developed man. The simple physical and social development of the individual produces change. The communication process, however imperfect, produces some change in both parties. However, when people or their environment are static, both the substance and the form of their communication tend to become stereotyped. Their talk may be reduced to limited and inconsequential matter. They may make much of little substance, gossip and repeat. The form may also take on a pattern, reflected in the terms of address, the places in which certain communication is appropriate, and the general establishment of rules and ritual that, in turn, affect substance. Where relationships between individuals are free and dynamic, there exists a continuing pressure to keep pace with others with whom we communicate. New content, about which there must be communication, develops, and new and changing forms or standards must be considered. These are reflected in the social situations, the job requirements, and the use of new media.

Societal Speech

If society is held together by communication, speech is the most essential and fundamental part of the adhesive. Throughout history human beings have remained together for the finding of food, the meeting of danger, the establishment of norms of conduct. In all these processes, activity has been coordinated by speech. The development of more complex group relationships has placed greater demands upon speech. In the broadest sense, the complexity of the group structure is dependent on the freedom, flexibility, and complexity of the communication. The importance of oral communication in goal determination, work specialization, establishment of value systems, capacity for aesthetic expression, development of symbols, adoption of rituals for spiritual and sentimental situations, and the planning of education for the young is self-evident. Speech is so vital a part of all this activity, so much a part of our lives, that it is taken for granted. Consider for a moment what would happen if all individuals in a particular community or geographic area were suddenly unable to speak. Whatever social, political, or economic organization exists would certainly be reduced in efficiency, if not destroyed, within a short time. If such an unfortunate condition affected the entire world, how long could the present level of our civilization be sustained?

It is evident that, as society becomes more complex, the role of speech develops a parallel significance and complexity. There are more persons, groups, things, and relationships about which it is necessary to talk. There are more alternatives and problems to consider, and the potentials for both good and ill change in importance and magnitude. More information—directions, appeals, feelings, and potentials—must be expressed in symbols. It is clearly impossible for all individuals to personally observe, experience, and come in direct contact with all that they must know even to survive. The ramifications of our dependency on others as we perform our daily vocational tasks defy simple analysis. To cope with all this complexity, we approximate direct experience through the medium of speech.

Some form of government is a characteristic of all social organization. In a free society such as ours, we have purposely founded that government on speech. It is the goal, form, and effect of such speech that is important in the democratic philosophy. Down through the ages all leaders, tyrants or democrats, have found it necessary to address the citizenry. It is thus that they explain, persuade, and exercise leadership. It is only in free societies that the people can and must talk freely and responsibly to those who operate their governments. This democratic concept places primary reliance on full, free, objective, and responsible expression by all members of the group. Truth and wisdom are expected to emerge as policy and program through the testing of ideas by the process of discussion and debate. The success of democracy depends on the development of a citizenry that assumes responsibility for being informed about, and for participating actively in, the affairs of government. Such responsibility can be assumed only by citizens who possess both knowledge of the principles and forms of speech and skill in the utilization of this knowledge in many situations and at all levels.

Thus it seems clear that the survival of a free society is dependent on the citizen performing the above functions effectively. Here, too, the circular speech cycle described earlier in the chapter may be seen in operation. The exchange between the citizen and his servant in government may not always be face-to-face or verbal; however, speech in both cases plays a basic role in determining the ideas that emerge in their various forms. The candidate for office presents his qualifications and platform, submits to questions, defends himself when attacked, and in turn criticizes and compares his opponent's platform to his own. The citizen-voter discusses issues with friends, attends informal meetings, listens to public speeches, reaches some conclusion, and acts accordingly. Unfortunately, his reaction sometimes is one of apathy or disgust, and he may withdraw from active participation. The officeholder—particularly at major administrative levels—holds meetings, seeks facts, attempts to gauge public sentiment, and prepares appeals and reports. The legislator conducts hearings and inquiries, debates issues in open session, and votes on matters of policy. Eventually, all representatives must return to the voter to explain their actions and to seek approval. This involved chain of communication is principally oral. The relationship of sender and receiver may not be so informal and the roles may not be reversed so frequently as in casual conversation, but such relationships must be preserved clearly and effectively if free men are to continue to determine their own destinies.

Just as the individual is in a state of constant dynamic adjustment, so, too, is the society in which the individual lives. A host of individuals and organizations constantly strive for change in the social pattern. The areas of concern range widely from economics to religion, and the potential effect may be major or minor. Not infrequently there are broad and basic differences of philosophy and purpose with which free societies must contend. Almost without exception, proposed changes are developed and presented by means of speech. Some person observes a problem that he feels merits action and discusses it informally with an acquaintance. Finding common interest, they talk to others of like mind, enlist aid, and discuss how best to proceed. Included in the plan of action is talk to persons who are in a position to provide support and take action —often, the voter. The proponents attempt to get all who are affected to talk about the problem and thus to develop a climate of public acceptance.

As the proposal comes to public attention, there will develop various degrees of interest, ranging from dedicated support to militant opposition. Soon those of contrary persuasion begin the parallel effort to communicate and organize, but with a different purpose. Finally, the problem is understood, the potential grasped, the advantages weighed, and action of some type results. Such is the pattern of behavior of free men, whether in an elementary or a complex social group—and common to all is the dependence on oral communication.

Vocational Speech

Paralleling the individual's adjustive and societal needs for oral communication are his vocational speech needs. Great economic and professional complexity characterize our contemporary society. Vast corporate structures not only provide innumerable products and services but exert great influence in many areas. Their multiple internal and external relationships present communication problems undreamed of in earlier times. As society provides increasingly more intensive training for professional and technical persons, the resulting specialization brings with it problems of communication. In addition, there is a continuous development of new occupations and areas of activity. The total result is a multiplication of communication problems. Individuals within a vocational area must seek to understand the objectives and functions of their organization or profession. As the quantity of knowledge within a field increases, specialized vocabularies develop to the point where in some cases only certain specialists are able to communicate with each other. The problems of external communication are equally critical.

While the public need not understand or appreciate all of the technical or specialized detail, it is they who ultimately must support, and in turn should be the beneficiaries of, such effort and knowledge. Thus there must be communication from the public and to the public. A notable example of this problem is the need for scientists to explain to the public concepts and implications of nuclear physics that were only suspected a decade ago. Whatever may be the situation—economic, scientific, or sociological—much of this communication must be oral, if for no other reason than that of the demands of speed and the fact that the volume of written material has passed the saturation point for the individual citizen. The result of this vocational and professional complexity is a marked increase in the variety and frequency of speech demands on both the individual and the group. In general, the vocational activities of our average citizen require him to meet and work with a wide range of individuals. He is expected to do this both on and off the job. He must have the ability to both give and receive information clearly, correctly, and efficiently. Frequently he will engage in group discussion. Often he will be in a position of either temporary or continuing leadership where he must generate enthusiasm in others; and, regardless of what he terms the activity, he is constantly engaged in informal debate—analyzing, supporting, attacking, and reaching conclusions about a policy or position. In a more specialized sense, people are called upon to supervise, interview, counsel, inspire, and persuade, all in the course of their economic or vocational activities.

As organizations develop, their nature, purpose, size, locations, and related factors affect the speech patterns and practices of their members. Questions arise concerning who talks to whom, when such communication is appropriate, and what specific individuals may talk about. The concepts of individuals in the organization, with respect to their personal worth, their job security, their social status, and their speech, become matters of great concern. In some situations it is considered necessary to adopt particular policies and patterns of oral communication. Both civilian and military organizations make extensive use of a form of oral presentation known as *briefing*. Many business organizations arrange meetings so that one or more major figures may speak to all possible employees. Closed-circuit television is sometimes used to help bridge distance in these cases. Many corporations make specific provision for group meetings, ranging from those involving production workers and supervisors through top management and on up into interorganizational committees and associations or professional conventions.

One characteristic of communication in contemporary society is the rise of parallel or competing groups to provide a means by which representatives of one organization may talk on somewhat equal terms to representatives of another organization. The employee of a large corporation finds it difficult if not impossible to identify, let alone communicate, with key individuals in that organization. One function of the modern labor union is to provide a vehicle by which such communication may take place. Again, the ultimate requirement is the same as we have observed in adjustive, societal, and governmental relations: increasing need for understanding of, and skill in, communication. Without such development, the channels of expression become closed, the individual becomes ineffectual and frustrated, and in the end society is also the loser.

Artistic Speech

It would be inappropriate to leave this discussion without recognizing that man uses speech as one important means of expressing his deepest and finest feelings. When he experiences and seeks to communicate such feelings, we may term his efforts "artistic speech." It is found in various forms of theater and may range from informal children's play to our greatest and most moving dramas. Sometimes verbal expression is combined with music, and we term this "opera" or "musical comedy." In another form, the individual may be reading prose or poetry, the latter finding its fullest meaning when read aloud by one who understands both the substance and the method. Certain of our mass media, such as radio and television, have utilized artistic speech in various forms and for a wide variety of purposes, often with commendable effects. In some situations, the audience may even be involved in a spontaneous manner. At times, the listener-receiver response is non-vocal. It may be intensely emotional; this is at least a part of the purpose of such communication. It is important to note that effective use of artistic speech requires superior skill in the integration of thought and expression. This is frequently achieved by careful and considered preparation of the message in written form—but, in each case, the final, effective expression is an oral one.

For varied purposes, then, ranging from basic survival to the expression of the most noble feelings, man utilizes a communicative relationship that is circular in nature and employs speech as its primary tool.

CHAPTER III

Speech and Education

General Objectives

Having treated the nature and role of speech in the preceding two chapters, let us consider the implications for education at all levels. How is this fundamental body of knowledge, attitudes, and skills to be included in the educational structure? Fortunately, experience, philosophy, and research provide sound guidelines. Education is dependent on communication, and a major share of this communication is speech. It has been estimated that between 85 and 90 per cent of all communication and of all learning takes place by speaking and listening. All formal, normal schooling is predicated on an educable child who can be taught to communicate with some degree of effectiveness. The first efforts of parents and teachers focus on training a child in the use of speech symbols. Most subsequent educational activity rests upon this foundation of language learning and application. As the child develops speech, he acquires the ability to manipulate symbols which he quickly learns to reduce to the sub-vocal speech that we term *thought*. Such sub-vocal speech constitutes a major portion of the thought process, however advanced may be the individual's ability to manipulate non-verbal symbols. Increase in human intelligence, therefore, requires a parallel increase in the type or complexity of the individual's symbol system—particularly, his speech-symbol system.

There is no question but that speech can and must be taught at all levels. Unfortunately, much of this teaching is poorly conceived, poorly organized, and sometimes harmful to the individual's communicative potential. Speech is not instinctive; it is learned. The child follows those models and patterns that he finds in his environment. Unconsciously and indirectly his parents, his teachers, and his peers provide the instruction. Thus, all social experiences continue to teach speech in one way or another. The question is—to what end and by what means? Research clearly demonstrates that the results of specific instruction in speech by qualified teachers are both positive and beneficial. As a result of such instruction, students speak more effectively. In addition to speech-skill modification, studies have revealed improvements in personality and in critical thinking.

The objectives of speech education are best viewed in three dimensions: concepts about the nature of speech; concepts concerning speech in human affairs; and concepts concerning speech as a humanistic study. Speech educators are in general agreement that all persons have need for, and should be helped to, speaking effectiveness. They recognize that there should be a common concern for all matters that touch upon the use and interpretation of the codes or symbols used in speaking. They see speech as an instrument of social adaptation, and they believe that all major forms of speaking should be included in the training program.

As an instrument of social utility, speech is concerned primarily and characteristically with questions of contingency or probability that do not lend themselves to exact determination at the moment. Thus, speech is used at both personal and group levels. Speech, as an instrument of utility, assumes the generation or existence of ideas worthy of consideration and communication. It envisions the selection and arrangement of materials concerning such ideas in the most effective and reasonable manner possible in order that there may be communication of such concepts to other individuals. It recognizes the importance of appropriate use of voice, action, and language as part of this process. The purpose of such communication is to achieve a dynamic adjustment between speakers and listeners.

There is also a special and significant body of material concerning speech as a humanistic or general study. Here speech is concerned with helping the individual to understand and deal with our common, as opposed to our personal, problems. This involves an appreciation of the universality of man's thoughts and feelings, his achievements and his failures. Important, of course, is an appreciation of the role that speech has played and can play in contributing to human understanding and progress. Such an approach to speech provides for experiences that are particularly rich and meaningful. The oral reading of prose and poetry opens the world of literature in a new dimension. Such considerations bring alive the dramatist's concepts, whether in the Greek tragedies, the plays of Shakespeare, or the works of contemporary writers. Of equal importance is the capacity to reveal the impact that oratory has had on the course of human thought and action. In every way, such a study provides opportunity to come into both intellectual and emotional contact with that which is most challenging, imaginative, and worthy in the thought of others.

What, then, are the objectives of speech education? The following is a partial list of the knowledge, attitudes, and skills that speech education seeks for the student:

1. Developing the ability to generate ideas about a subject and to investigate the sources of pertinent information so as to gather systematically the necessary materials for oral discourse.
2. Arranging and, ultimately, selecting the materials to be used in light of the subject, the audience, and the total complex situation in which oral communication will take place.
3. Selecting and organizing the material in terms of an appropriate specific objective to be achieved.
4. Thinking about both the content and the presentation of the message so as to consider fully, objectively, and critically all the elements and alternatives.
5. Casting of messages or statements in language that is clear, appropriate, accurate, pictorial, and impelling.
6. Presenting oral communication effectively and appropriately by means of (a) physical behavior that reflects self-control, poise, confidence, sincerity, and individuality, and (b) vocal behavior that reflects control, clarity, audibility, flexibility, and pleasantness.
7. Learning to observe the effects of the speech in the total situation and to modify continuing communication behavior accordingly.
8. Learning to listen to other speakers attentively, intelligently, and critically.
9. Developing the capacity to understand, respond to, and interpret literature through oral reading and acting, with sensitivity to both the intellectual and the emotional elements, as well as to the literary form.
10. Understanding the nature of group discussion and developing the ability to participate in its varying forms while managing effectively both the substance and the interpersonal aspects.
11. Understanding the nature and purpose of advocacy, including the treatment of controversial ideas by debate and persuasion.
12. Understanding and practicing ethical standards in all speaking situations.

13. Assisting the individual to discover his speech needs, abilities, and problems, and helping him to gain insight regarding these.
14. Acquiring attitudes toward self and toward others that contribute to effective speaking and listening. Included are such attitudes as (a) willingness to participate in oral communication, (b) willingness to accept the relationships that characterize speaker-listener interaction, and (c) belief in the potential of speech for improving human understanding and relationships.

Adaptation to Student Maturation

How is a program aimed at achieving these objectives to be adapted to the contemporary school and the pupils it serves? In planning the total program, there are certain fundamental principles to be observed. All students should receive instruction in speech, beginning as early as possible and continuing throughout the period of formal education. In general, such instruction should recognize and treat speech as a separate and distinct subject or discipline. At all levels both the teacher and the student should understand that the purpose of such training is to provide useful information about oral communication and to provide graded and guided experience in all basic or fundamental aspects of speaking situations. They must understand that this study deals with the most fundamental needs and abilities that man possesses; it is not concerned merely with mechanical skills and artificial forms. In providing a program adapted to the abilities and maturity of all students, proper diagnosis and supervised practice aimed at correcting handicaps and eliminating undesirable habits and patterns of speech would be included. Practice intended to improve speech skills should be based on immediate needs and interests, and adequate facilities and equipment should be available at all times.

The elementary level provides opportunity for efficient and effective instruction based upon the foregoing principles. In the early grades, most children are readily stimulated to communicate; they address their expression to matters concerning self and the interrelationship of self with others. This provides opportunity for expansion of the child's world of ideas and relationships. Speech may serve as an outlet for, and also a stimulus to, imagination and creativity. Some of the most functional speech situations may be introduced, such as the management of conversation, the use of the telephone, extending and accepting invitations, and the presentation of some types of reports. Both impromptu and planned dramatic activities can be employed. Puppets can be used effectively. Individual oral reading and choric speaking can be used.

Informal speech situations are everywhere. With increasing student maturity, advantage may be taken of the opportunity to channel effort into informative speeches involving reports and original ideas, interpretations, and beliefs. Student committees may undertake to plan and execute projects. Through such experiences, students may come to understand the nature of group discussion and the sharing of responsibility. With increasing age and experience, the elementary student may gain confidence in his ability and skill in planning and conducting meetings, assemblies, and public programs. Certainly the elementary level provides the opportune time for the discovery and correction of speech and hearing defects. Not only are the immediate and observable dividends from resources expended greatest at this point, but early correction of handicaps may make available additional years of normal communication and development for the child. The need for early therapy is essential in light of the effect that limited, defective, or inappropriate speech has upon both personality and social adjustment.

All this will not be achieved without trained personnel, enlightened classroom teachers, and administrative cooperation. Effective teaching of speech is one of the most difficult and complex challenges that the elementary-school teacher faces. To even approach the great potential available at this level requires teachers who are prepared to teach speech in the same way that they are prepared to teach science, social studies, music, or many other subject areas.

The junior high school years are characterized by the development of curiosity, the expansion of intellectual horizons, and changes in maturity. All these may be used constructively in the program of speech education. Where speech instruction in the elementary school will generally be integrated into the total daily or weekly program, at the junior high level the focus should be more specific. One alternative is to organize the instruction around the elements of speech, including the concept of communication as a complex human activity. Another is to approach the subject through speech activities or the forms of speaking. A third possibility is the combination of the preceding approaches. A minimum program would involve the establishment of speech as a separate course, as well as coordination or follow-up to insure that the knowledge and skills presented were being used effectively in other subject areas and student activities. This would require at least one semester each year—preferably, two semesters.

Whatever the organization and time allotment, the instruction should emphasize individual expression of ideas. Such expression should be based on specific training in discovering, selecting, arranging, and presenting material within the framework of good oral communication. In addition, instruction should utilize group projects and activities with increased frequency. Opportunities should be sufficiently numerous and varied as to involve all students. Specific attention should be given to discover the strengths and diagnose the difficulties of individual students, as well as to plan programs for the improvement and evaluation of their work. Since students at this level will vary widely in maturity and motivation, it is important to differentiate instruction so as to challenge the individual student.

In general, increasing opportunity and responsibility should be extended to the student as he progresses through the speech curriculum. At this point in the instructional program, the work in speech may be effectively related to the objectives of self-realization and effective human relations. Units of the specific courses, projects, and programs will include public speaking, reading, both informal and formal discussion and debate, dramatic activities, and parliamentary procedure. Many opportunities present themselves for extracurricular applications and activities, including participation in Parent-Teacher Association programs and the judicious use of competition, both within the school and between schools. The junior high school is a period in the student's physical and psychological development where his drive for adjustment and self-expression is extremely high. The careful planning and intelligent direction of a program of speech instruction at that level can do much to help young boys or girls to understand themselves, to find constructive outlets for their tremendous interest and energy, and to contribute to their improved performance in other areas of the curriculum.

The senior high school should build upon the preceding programs and should provide increased differentiation based on individual needs, interests, and abilities. This suggests a sequence of basic course offerings, as well as specialized and enriched supplementary courses. A program for all students should include one or more of the following: a required course in speech fundamentals or required integrated units of speech fundamentals coupled with applications in other classes, or units of speech fundamentals integrated within a broader program such as language arts, communications courses, core curricula, or common-learning programs. For students with special interests and superior abilities, there should be elective courses such as public speaking, oral interpretation, dramatics, discussion and debate, and radio-television. Such students should also have additional opportunities in co-curricular speech activities, including forensics, dramatics, speakers' bureau programs, radio-television workshops, and the like. Students who continue to suffer from speech or hearing handicaps necessitating ongoing clinical attention should be discovered and diagnosed through speech surveys conducted as part of the basic program initiated in the elementary grades and carried on through all subsequent levels. These students should receive assistance from qualified therapists who coordinate their efforts with classroom instructors.

College and university instruction in speech should provide for both a generalized and an intensive study of the discipline. At this level, speech may be termed the study of man through an examination of his communicative behavior. Such a concept emphasizes the liberal or humanistic aspects of the subject and recognizes the universality of the communication process. Speech, viewed in this light, embraces a body of knowledge at least equal in value to that found in any other discipline. Such a view accommodates both the functional and the artistic aspects of speech and makes possible the development of personal proficiency.

Another, and often coordinated, view of speech is that of professional or vocational training. A familiar example is the inclusion of one or more designated speech courses in a curriculum that is not primarily focused on speech. Where this is true, the most common purpose is to provide some basic knowledge and also to develop abilities and attitudes that will be useful to the individual in his chosen vocation. Such is the justification for requiring courses in public speaking and discussion for majors in business, engineering, forestry, or medicine. Some familiarity with radio and television is generally recognized as being necessary for the well-trained journalist. A requirement in speech is becoming increasingly common for majors in education, English, political science, psychology, and sociology. Under certain circumstances, special courses are developed to meet particular needs. In this direction lies the danger that such highly specialized adaptation may approach training as contrasted with education. Whatever the arrangement, a significant amount of interdepartmental and interdisciplinary service is provided through the basic foundation courses.

For students seriously interested in the field, specific curricula are designed to provide preparation for careers in some area of communication or in vocations where such training is of great value. Many majors in speech find positions as classroom teachers at all levels. Special programs for rehabilitation of the handicapped are generally accepted as part of our education system and attract increasing numbers of students. In addition to standards imposed by the profession, most states have basic requirements for certification of teacher-therapists. The number of students finding careers in radio and television, or theater, is increasing. There is also a growing demand for specialists in communication to work in large or complex organizations, and many students major in speech as preparation for continuing study in law, business administration, industrial relations, or technical and scientific communications. As speech finds a community of interest with, and draws from, many fields, so it contributes to many areas of human endeavor. Whatever the area of specialization, graduates in speech have increasingly broad and rich training of an interdisciplinary nature.

At the college and university level, the most common and often the most effective administrative arrangement provides for a separate department within a college of liberal arts. At the present time, most of the stronger and more progressive programs have developed under such an arrangement. In some instances, fragmentation has occurred where the community of interest has been obscured, where excessive specialization has developed, or where the size of the administrative unit has become unwieldy. The nature and scope of course offerings inevitably depend in some degree on the nature or purpose of the institution. However, the range of courses will generally recognize the unique needs of both the student and the areas within the field. The basic course commonly focuses either on fundamentals or on public speaking. Specialized courses may cover a variety of areas, such as public address, drama, interpretation, speech science, broadcasting, communication theory, speech education, and speech pathology and audiology.

Activities or public performances are frequently coordinated or integrated with the curricular offerings. Student participation may be required or voluntary, and credit may or may not be granted for such involvement. Customarily, all students interested, able, and willing to put forth the necessary effort may seek to participate, although opportunity is seldom guaranteed for all. An "open door" policy of this nature serves to make certain features of the speech instructional program available to a wider segment of the student body on a non-class basis. Such programs should be supervised by a qualified faculty member who has competence and interest in the special area and who has both adequate time and appropriate recognition of the significance of this supervisory responsibility as an integral part of his teaching function.

At the graduate level, both the scope and the quality of the training have increased significantly. At the present time, most major universities offer a master's program and many offer the doctorate in speech and theater. The general objectives are to conduct both basic and applied research concerning the process of human communication, to improve the teaching of speech at all levels, and to prepare specialists to work in various areas of the broad field.

In addition to the inclusion of speech requirements in vocational curricula at both the secondary and the college level, there is a growing recognition of the importance of speech in the adult world. This stems from a variety of motivations on the part of many different elements in our population. The academic response to an expressed need has ranged from organized adult learning courses to specific postgraduate programs for groups in business, labor, the military, and the professions. Maturity and experience bring to many a sense of personal inadequacy in oral communication coupled with an increasing awareness of the importance and complexity of the communication process. Experience, including both success and failure, brings to many a realization of the critical role that speech plays in vocational success. Typical of those wishing general knowledge and broad orientation are executives, teachers, religious workers, nurses and doctors, military officers, labor leaders, and government employees. More specific assistance in such specialized areas as persuasion, debate, discussion techniques, parliamentary procedure, or communication theory is frequently sought by salesmen, candidates for public office, and organizational leaders or officers. In many urban and some rural areas, cultural activities generate needs for speech training. This involves persons affiliated with community service projects, adult learning or discussion groups, community theaters, youth clubs, and related organizations.

Such diversity of interests and needs often calls for individual adaptations, focusing on special content and activities. In some circumstances, emphasis is placed on informal speaking, including interviewing, round table discussion, and book reviewing. Certain forms of public address, such as public speaking, parliamentary procedure, and persuasion, are popular with other groups. Large organizations in all areas of our cultural complex—social, economic, governmental, and religious—are increasingly concerned that both workers and leaders understand the principles, practices, and problems of communication that are unique to specific organizational structures. Related to this is the growing concern with scientific-technical information in all of its ramifications. Broadcasting is so much a part of our contemporary life that the organization leader or spokesman must be familiar with this medium and prepared to utilize it effectively. As available leisure time increases, there is more opportunity for informal community groups to work in the theater. Parents, particularly mothers, will join together frequently in the study of speech development in children.

Our contemporary concepts lead us to see education as a never-ending process in which the total resources of the organized educational system are continuously involved. Thus, the speech teacher, curriculum planner, and educational administrator must be legitimately concerned with serving—in one way or another—the needs of the adult and with relating this part of the total program to the formally organized instructional curriculum. It is not uncommon that the adults who feel a need for speech improvement are unaware of the resources available, the nature of the programs required, and the problems and potentials involved in improving their oral communication. Sometimes existing courses, at either the secondary or the college level, will meet their needs and obviously should be employed. Where new programs or arrangements are required, they should be built upon an educationally sound foundation. The level of instruction and the complexity of content may vary from high school to postgraduate work; and the scope may vary from a single contact covering a few hours or a day to a continuing program over a period of months or even years.

The method of organizing such instruction depends on the diversity of personnel, the existent needs, and the available resources. One possibility provides the student an opportunity to enroll, for credit or no credit, for courses already in existence. A second possibility is the development of a course of instruction for a group of individuals in a field, such as members of a professional, business, or labor organization. A third possibility is the planning of a semi-specialized program open to any who wish to enroll, without regard to their backgrounds or areas of work. This is a procedure employed with such courses as parliamentary procedure, discussion and conference leadership, and public speaking—to name just a few. Sometimes an organization or business will arrange for a special program or group of programs to be made available to selected groups of individuals within the organization. At other times a special consulting arrangement may be established for the purpose of assisting a particular individual to attack a limited problem or to explore a specific communication situation. Finally, there is the arrangement that includes a specialized speech or communication section within the broad training program of an organization or enterprise. Such breadth and flexibility would not ordinarily be possible within a formal curricular program, but it is quite common and proper where individuals and organizations can work cooperatively with specialists in speech to locate and attack problems in a reasonable order of priority and on an educationally justifiable basis.

Whatever may be the nature of the adult students involved, the content to be considered, or the administrative arrangements, at least three qualities will characterize effective programs for adults. First, there is a recognition of and an adaptation to the backgrounds and needs of the group being served. Second, there is in addition adaptation of procedures to the particular situation and personnel. Finally, there must exist on the part of the teacher special personality attributes and attitudes that make it possible for him to understand the adult and his problems, to establish effective rapport, to make possible mutual respect, and to work cooperatively in an interesting and challenging common project.

Teacher Preparation

The role of speech in education is not limited to the pupil and his mastery of the subject matter of speech. The teacher of any subject is, first and foremost, a communicator who, regardless of his subject field, should possess a knowledge of speech theory and more than average skill in using a wide variety of speech forms. Unfortunately, too little is known about the specific nature of teacher communication; but empirical evidence and specific research studies indicate that competence in speech is one of the principal factors that correlate with teacher success in the field. Mention was made earlier of the increasing frequency with which colleges of education are including a demonstration of adequacy in speech as a part of the requirement for graduation. However organized or wherever included, preparation for meeting this requirement should call for a basic understanding of the nature and function of speech, coupled with appreciation of, and skill in, informal communication, group discussion, public speaking, and reading aloud. The effective teacher must also be trained in listening and must have developed the ability to use feedback as an essential part of the teaching process.

Where the teacher has special responsibilities or particular subject areas, additional theory and practical skill may be required. Teachers at the elementary level need to understand the nature of speech development in children and the role of the speech pathologist and audiologist in the school program. The social studies are particularly rich in problems that lend themselves to discussion and debate; teachers of social studies should have knowledge of these particular forms of public address. Teachers of English may benefit from work in interpretation and dramatics; it is not uncommon to find that the effective teacher of literature has a minor, and sometimes a joint major, in speech.

If the above are guidelines for the preparation of teachers in other subject-matter areas, what should be the training of the teacher of speech? The basic preparation should be characterized by breadth. This would suggest courses in speech physiology and psychology, voice and articulation, forms of public address, interpretation, and drama, coupled with methods of teaching speech and some knowledge of the objectives and problems of the speech pathologist and audiologist. Specialization in the foregoing or related areas can then proceed as interest and need dictate. Cognate or minor areas of study might include one or more of the following: social psychology, language and literature, and one or more of the social studies. Extensive experience in speech activities outside the classroom should be a part of the teacher's training. While the individual's interest may be primarily in forensics or dramatics, whenever possible the elementary and secondary teacher should have some knowledge of both areas. Post-collegiate enrichment and experience should be gained from involvement in appropriate activities on a personal basis. These might include involvement in professional organizations, civic activities, or participation in political party work. Thus, the teacher may enlarge his perspective and gain insight into the application of the theory that he teaches in his classroom. The teacher of speech who shuns such involvement may be compared to the teacher of geology who never goes into the field.

The individual teacher cannot, and should not, bear the entire burden of responsibility for establishing and maintaining appropriate standards of effective oral communication. Local schools, professional societies, and accrediting agencies should cooperate in establishing minimum standards to be met by all. This is particularly critical in the area of speech and theater because of our fallacious assumption that our present standards of performance are adequate and our tendency to take speech competence for granted. The result is that in some instances present minima are so low as to be relatively meaningless. The effect of the present North Central Association requirement of five semester hours of college credit in speech as a basis for approving teachers in this subject degrades the discipline, the students enrolled in the subject, and the teachers responsible for their instruction. Most school systems with respectable curricula in speech require that the teacher have the equivalent of an undergraduate speech major. A suggested minimum standard for the teacher at the junior or senior high school level would be such a major built upon the foundation outlined above, with recognition of the need for specialization in particular areas.

The general preparation of the elementary-school teacher should include a number of foundation courses in speech, supplemented by special work dealing with speech development and elementary speech correction. Additional courses might well come as graduate work beyond the B. A. degree. As the teacher of speech gains experience and assumes increasing responsibility for course and curriculum development, graduate work will be necessary in speech and related areas. Such demands are consistent with the forward thrust of knowledge and the raising of standards everywhere evident. They find additional justification in the point made earlier, that the teacher of speech, at whatever level, has one of the most complex and difficult tasks of all teachers in the school system.

Ethical Considerations

The role of speech in personality development and social interaction is so important that it is impossible, in any thoroughgoing sense, to consider its relationship to the processes of education without paying attention to the value concepts of society and of the individuals who function within the society. It is not essential to the present discussion to attempt to delineate what these value concepts are or should be. To focus attention on the significance and the desirability of careful deliberation on this matter, however, there will be value in considering some specifics of the relationship of speech to education that possess clear, ethical implications. Among these a more or less arbitrary choice can be made of the speaker's obligation to an audience, the oral interpreter's obligations as a communicator, the merits of debating both sides of a question, and the nature of dramatic distortion. Such a choice is not only limited; it makes no pretense at representativeness. It serves merely to illustrate the fact that ethical considerations exist and demand attention.

What is the speaker's obligation to his audience? Is the speaker's responsibility purely to himself? Should speech education seek to develop fluency, effective organization, the ability to inform and to persuade independent of the truth or of the best interests of the people whose concepts, convictions, and actions the speaker seeks to influence? If the answer to this is in the negative, if students are to be taught not only to be communicative but to communicate within the context of personal and social responsibility, then who is to determine what particular context should be encouraged? Is it enough to teach a student that his public speaking must relate to an ethical value system, that of necessity it cannot help but do so? Or is it an essential part of speech education to guide the student into a more conscious awareness of what that value system should be? Speech education is viewed throughout this monograph as an essential part of training the citizen to function in a democracy; but speech plays a vital role in meeting the communication needs of nondemocratic cultures as well.

If it is true that the public speaker cannot help but relate to an ethical value system, may it not also be true that speech education cannot help but establish such a relationship? If we consider the educational significance of example and of environment, what is the impact on the student of the way speech is utilized within the educational environment in which he is trained? What is the effect of participation in student-government organizations set up to provide experience in the use of certain decision-making machinery but carefully restricted so as to prevent the students from dealing with any decisions of importance? What is the effect of a basically authoritarian educational complex in which severe and obvious limitations are placed on the freedom of expression and on the participation in decision-making of the teachers, including those who teach speech? These questions cannot be ignored; to attempt to ignore them is, in a very real sense, one way of answering them.

Moving on to another illustration, what is the responsibility of the oral interpreter of literature to the author of that literature, and how does this relate to the interpreter's personal communicative objectives? Should the teacher of interpretation recognize the fact that intimate and prolonged contact with a significant work of literature can help the student to grow in insight and sensitivity? And should the teacher of interpretation take advantage of this recognition by assigning to the student for reading specific literary selections that will contribute most beneficially to the personality needs of the student? Or is this a form of practicing psychiatry without proper qualifications? What is the communicative objective of interpretation within an educational framework? Does the objective relate back to the personality needs of the student interpreter? Is the interpreter's entire effort to be aimed at sharing a literary appreciation of an author's work? Or is the student to be encouraged to seek a communicative impact on the audience that reflects his own values and his own informational and persuasive objectives, and that utilizes skill in interpretation as a powerful means to his communicative ends? Such questions cannot be divorced from questions concerning the inherent values of oral interpretation and of literature.

A third illustration may be taken from the area of debate. Here the question has been raised as to the implications and consequences of asking students to debate both sides of a question. Does the student who debates both sides of a question profit by a resultant understanding of the question that exceeds what he could derive from debating only one side? Does the way to effective persuasion pass through the experience of understanding the views of those whom you seek to persuade? And does arguing the other man's cause provide the best insight into his point of view? Will the experience of debating both sides of a question make a student more tolerant of conflicting viewpoints by bringing him to the realization that there are strong arguments on the side of those whose convictions are opposed to his own? Or is the American educational system already too strongly oriented in the direction of producing students who equate tolerance and broad-mindedness with the ability to see both sides of any question to the point where they have no conviction, arrive at no personal sense of commitment, and avoid taking a positive public stand on any controversial issue? Does arguing both sides of a question foster a glorification of sophistry—of slick, fluent persuasion divorced from personal conviction? Does the student who gets up before an audience and urges this audience to accept a position that he himself rejects experience—however unconsciously—a deterioration of his own standards of integrity? Can a student be oriented to view the choice of the side he is to argue in a debate as simply part of an intellectual learning exercise with no more moral implications than are involved in the decision as to whether, in the chess tournament, he is to play with the white pieces or the black? And if a student can be so oriented, is such an orientation desirable?

A final illustration is provided by the distortion of life that may be inherent in any theatrical activity and that is in no way lessened by the fact that the activity is described as educational. Plato objected to art as imitation on the grounds that imitation was a poor substitute for reality. Aristotle's defense was that the artist was selective and that, as a result, many people could achieve insights from a work of art that they were too insensitive or imperceptive to achieve from the reality that was being imitated. But one may question whether the nature of the selectivity of theater art does not all too often result in an insight that is fallacious. The search for what is dramatic leads the playwright to focus on climactic moments and to compress the time intervals between such moments. As a result, the theater often presents what is not so much an intensified or vivified picture of life as it is an exciting contact with what is undoubtedly intense and vivid but unrelated to the actualities of life. In contrast with what occurs in the theater, life often seems pallid. The student brought up on a steady diet of theater may find little to entice him in the everyday fare of his daily existence, or he may devote his time and energies to preparing himself for a life that has no actual existence outside the theater. Perhaps the greatest danger is that the student who has learned to react to the relatively blatant impact of theatrical climax situations may become insensitive to the dramatic impact and implications of the more subtle crisis and climax situations with which he comes into personal contact.

The preceding illustrations are designed to raise questions rather than to present answers. To accomplish this, the discussions have been inconclusive and, perhaps, frustratingly circuitous. The point is a simple one: both the student and the teacher of speech and theater must confront the ethical dimensions of their activity.

CHAPTER IV

Theater

The Nature of Theater

Actor and audience are the essential ingredients in theater. The actor brings a character to life before the audience. The actor normally works with other actors, and the characters are normally involved in a conflict situation that progresses to a climax and a resolution. Most frequently, what the actors do and say is based on a manuscript. The word *theater* labels a cultural activity with a long history and a vast multitude of participants. The label may also refer to the physical environment in which the actors and the audience assemble. Finally, it may describe the process of interaction between the actors and the audience at that moment when the script is being brought to life.

Although a script in complete written form is common to contemporary theatrical practice, it is not inherently necessary. Actors may work from a rough-plot outline or from the barest description of characterization and initial conflict situation, with the vast bulk of the action and dialogue left to their abilities of improvisation. Whatever is brought to life before the eyes of the audience may be defined as *theater* or, quite commonly, as a *play*. The *play* is often reserved, as a term, to describe the script from which the actors worked or the script that might be composed as a record of what they said and did. This play script may, although it often does not, possess real literary merit, in which case it is properly considered to be *dramatic literature*. *Drama* often refers to such literature or to the theater that comes into existence when such literature is brought to life before an audience. What the audience responds to in its participation in a theatrical experience is usually the result of some preparation. The preparation process is often designated by the term *production*. *Production* may involve the coordination of the activity of a great many different people with a wide variety of talents. These distinctions are meaningful and necessary, although the terminology is neither precise nor universal.

Theatrical production can be undertaken in response to a number of motivations. As a speech art, theater provides an excellent training and testing situation for vocal control and expressiveness. If anything, the situation it provides is more rigorous as a test than it is effective as training. Such a relationship is suggested, at least, by the large number of actors who continue to fail the test after considerably lengthy periods of the training. It should be apparent that the theater exists, as a speech art, only for the benefit of the actor. A person may engage in acting or be encouraged to act with this type of personal development in view. Many actors have other objectives, however, such as are discussed below. Obviously, the theater involves many who are not actors. The total theater activity, therefore, must not be limited to providing training in speech.

As a liberal art, theater provides a vivid and unique contact with an extensive body of literature. The significance of this literature is attested to by the eminence given to dramatists in any listing of the great writers of the world. Consider what the status of world literature would be if it did not include the works of the dramatists, of such writers as Sophocles, Shakespeare, Molière, Chekhov, and Shaw, to name only a few. Since dramatic literature was created with theatrical production in mind, the full appreciation of this literature and the capacity to experience the richest response to it would seem to call for an opportunity to react to it in the theater— whatever additional opportunities to react to it might exist. This value exists for the members of the audience. For those who participate in the production, there are additional benefits. Production provides the motivation to undertake a detailed study of the literature and to conduct the study with constant reference to the artistic medium for which the literature was designed.

As a fine art, theater provides the instruments that are utilized by interpretative artists to bring to an audience the impact of a dramatist's composition. As a fine art, theater combines the best efforts of artists wholly dedicated to their art. This insistence on complete absorption in the creative and interpretative process on the part of highly talented artists striving for the maximum of artistic effectiveness is the major identifying characteristic of theater as a fine art.

As a commercial venture, theater provides experiences of sufficient interest and value to the members of the audience for them to be willing to pay for benefits received. When payment is sufficient to support those involved in production and to provide a return to those who have invested in the production financially, commercial theater is successful.

As recreation, theater provides members of a community the opportunity to obtain the satisfaction of making a cultural contribution to the community at large. The process of play production is a creative one, it is socially enjoyable—or can be—and it is distinctly different from the normal routines of the lives most people live. Recreational theater also provides opportunity for the activity of people with other motivations. In the recreational theater, adults may continue their liberal educations and aspiring artists may develop their talents. For the members of the audience, all theater may be recreational.

The theater of the actor and audience existed long before the emergence of writing and quite possibly before the emergence of speech. Indeed, if men had any motivation to communicate in a narrative sense prior to the development of language, acting out the narrative would seem to be a natural solution to the communicative problem. This is a method still available and utilized by people possessing no common language of speech. Whatever its origins in the dim and distant past, theater has flourished from exceedingly primitive times into our own day. The tradition of theatrical practice, criticism, and history is as old as our knowledge of man as a social creature. Theater has permeated almost all cultures in all parts of the world at all stages of human development. So extensive is the scope of theater that its systematic study requires a tremendous breadth of knowledge.

In its fullest development, theater is an exceedingly complex art—somewhat unique in that it combines not only artists but also a variety of arts. The members of an audience who respond to a contemporary theatrical production focus their attention on the work of the actor, who brings a character to life before them. The illusion created by the actor, however, is facilitated by the artistic contributions of many others. The actor speaks and acts as guided by a written script produced by the playwright, whose art is essentially literary. The actor appears in costumes that are the combined products of a costume designer and a costume maker. The actor is seen in a specific setting created by scenic and lighting designers and craftsmen. The actor may be aided by sound ranging from door buzzers through thunderstorms to mood music. The actor employs make-up. All these arts, crafts, and effects assist the actor to interpret the script.

The actor is also involved in integrating his efforts with those of other actors. In this integration, the actor is assisted by the director. The director may function as an aid to the actor, providing the benefit of a different vantage point. The director may function quite differently, however, viewing himself as the artist primarily responsible for the interpretation of the script and considering the actor one of the elements available to him in his interpretative activity. Both points of view, as well as many intermediary ones, can be found in the theater.

In addition to the audience and the production artists, craftsmen, and technicians, theater involves others. The theater architect may be considered as one of these, although most theaters are probably designed by architects who have not specialized in this type of architecture—a fact that is frequently most unfortunately obvious to those whose activity in the theater takes them beyond the auditorium where the audience is seated. Among others involved are the critic, the historian, the scholar, and the teacher.

The critic has performed a variety of functions, with individual critics differing as to which specific function or functions they undertook to perform. One simple task undertaken by the critic is to sample a theatrical production and report on his responses for the benefit of others who were considering whether or not to join the audience. This task is so simple, perhaps, as to be better labelled *reviewing* than dignified by the title of *criticism*. The critic also serves as an evaluator, basing his evaluations on a much more profound study and a much more extensive background of knowledge than is commonly true of the reviewer. The critic also engages in analysis designed to increase the understanding and the appreciation of the subject of the criticism. What might be described as *criticism in depth* is time-consuming and not well adapted to those elements of theater that are transitory. Such criticism, therefore, tends to focus most on the dramatic literature which, in its purely literary form, is available for close scrutiny over a sustained period.

In addition, however, such criticism can and has focused on theater as an art or as a social force within a given culture.

The historian seeks to record theater activity and to reconstruct the theater activity of earlier periods from the historical remnants left behind. Historical remnants might include such items as scripts; prompt books; scene, costume, or building designs; financial records; diary entries; letters; the fading memories of "old-timers" or relatives; newspaper clippings; playbills; and archeological remains. The sources are many and varied and much ingenuity and knowledge is necessary to move from one clue to the next. For some people, the task of historical reconstruction is exciting and fascinating.

The scholar seeks to enlarge the body of knowledge concerning the theater. The historian of the theater is such a scholar; but theatrical scholarship extends beyond the area of historical reconstruction. Numerous subjects may be investigated. For example, a student of the theater might undertake to analyze the techniques and aesthetic theory of a specific playwright, or director, or school of acting. Another suitable subject could be analysis of audience-response patterns or of variations in audience responses under a variety of circumstances, such as differences of geographical location or socioeconomic status or sex or education. Another suitable subject could be an analysis of the criteria employed in play-script evaluation by writers' agents, established actors, directors, and reviewers. Still another subject suited to investigation could be an analysis of the problems involved in the adaptation of literature into various dramatic forms for stage, television, or film. A host of other possibilities exist; this should suffice to point up the fact that theatrical scholarship is far wider in scope than what is normally considered within the province of the theater historian.

The teacher can seek to develop skill in the practice of theater, including the practice of theatrical criticism and theatrical scholarship. The teacher can also strive to enlarge the student's understanding and appreciation of the theater, concerning himself with students who may have no intention of ever participating in theater activity in any capacity other than as members of an audience.

The study of theater has definitely established a place for itself in the academic community. The manner in which it is undertaken is dependent on the educational objectives. These objectives vary.

This is reflected in the fact that theater study is undertaken within such academic divisions as Colleges of Liberal Arts and Sciences, Colleges and Schools of Fine Arts, Schools of Speech, and Graduate Schools.

The Theater Process

The production of a play based on a script begins with the work of a playwright. The playwright writes with the interpretative artists and the machinery of the theater in mind; but he writes in response to his own communicative desires with respect to his audience. The playwright's creativity, like that of any creative artist, may be triggered in many ways. The playwright may start with a philosophical concept, a particular locale, a group of characters, a conflict situation, a bit of dialogue, or an intriguing title. What the playwright ends with is a script that reveals a group of characters involved in a conflict situation within a particular environment. The revelation is achieved through action and dialogue that can be presented to an audience within the theater. Most commonly, the conflict is intensified during the progress of the plot and is worked out so as to be consistent with the personalities and the motivations of the characters involved. The conflict moves to a climax, at which point the audience comes to share the playwright's basic insight. To understand the communicative dimension of a play script, it is necessary to understand the climax in terms of this basic insight. This basic insight may be profound; it certainly need not be. This insight is common to all play scripts that have a meaningful communicative dimension, whether they be tragedies, farces, melodramas, comedies, or musicals.

The interpretative artists of the theater unify their production efforts by relating all of their activity to an agreed-upon understanding of the basic insight established in the climax. In developing characterizations, in employing light, color, fabric, visual composition, patterns and rhythms of movement for the establishment of mood, in integrating music and all the elements that make up the production complex, the interpretative artists seek to make the climax clear and powerful in its impact on the audience. All that precedes the climax is seen as contributing to the clarity or emotional intensity of the climax itself. If the interpretative artists are successful, the climax will affect the audience as the point of maximum emotional impact. In other words, the audience will focus maximum attention at the point of climax. If the playwright is successful, the insight given to the audience at this point will reward the attention and justify the energies expended in gaining it.

The inability to make the point of insight correspond with the point of maximum emotional impact may result from a weakness in the writing too great to be overcome by the interpretative artists. Even where the writing is sound in this regard, however, the desired impact does not come of itself. The work of the individual interpretative artist is difficult work, as is the process of integrating the work of all the artists involved. The production process, therefore, includes a long period of preparation. Personnel must be chosen with the play script in mind. While the business end of the theater is being taken care of, the play is mounted, technically, and the actors and director go into rehearsal. The three activities are closely interrelated. Management considerations will determine such factors as the physical theater situation in which the play is to be performed, the scenic and costume possibilities or limitations, the availability of an orchestra, and even the selection of a particular play script. There must be complete integration among designers, technicians, actors, and director concerning such matters as period, style, mood, and purpose. As a specific instance, it is apparent that the scene designer cannot draw plans for construction and the director cannot block the movement of the actors until the scene designer and the director have agreed as to the floor plan.

Although there are deviations in the practices of various directors or producing groups, the rehearsal process can be described as following—quite frequently—a fairly regular sequence. The actors study the script, analyzing their individual roles and the function of each role with respect to the play as an entity. Actors and director come together on certain basic concepts, although refinements of understanding will come throughout the production process. The action is blocked; that is, the actors' movements into, within, and out of the acting area are planned. As the actors go through their movements on stage, they mark the action in their play scripts. Then follows a period of working on refinements in vocal and physical interpretation, within the limitations imposed by the necessity for the actors to handle scripts. In the repetitive working on line delivery and physical delineation of character, the actors become much more familiar with what they must say and do. Several repetitions tend to fix the actions sufficiently so that the actors need not refer to the directions they have placed in their scripts.

Memorization of lines usually requires intensive individual study outside rehearsal time. A few rehearsals can be devoted to helping the actors free themselves of the scripts. There comes a time when actors are expected to work without scripts but with occasional prompting, and then with neither script nor assistance. This is a difficult task that may be facilitated by staggering the times at which the several parts of the play must be freed of dependence on the script. In staggering the time schedule for memorization, however, care must be taken to avoid uneven preparation of the various portions.

Once the actors are free of the script, the production can really begin to move toward performance. While the attention to fine points of delivery and action is never abandoned, the prime focus can now shift to integration, stylization, emotional build, and timing. The problems are now almost orchestral in nature. When the production group works with a new script that is being revised as part of the production process, the major revision should be completed prior to this stage of rehearsal. When the parts seem to be fitting together well, the technical elements are introduced. This is facilitated by very early use of mock elements, such as a stick for the sword or a chair for the throne.

There is a point at which a rehearsal can be held that is clearly stipulated as being a technical rehearsal. The actors "walk and talk" their way through the play. They do not try to act; such an attempt would be frustrating to them and they would look upon the technical elements as an intrusion to be resented rather than an aid to be appreciated. The purpose of the technical rehearsal is to integrate technical elements with the work of the actors. Usually this is primarily a matter of sequence and timing. For example, the sound man comes to know precisely how much time exists between his ringing of the telephone and his starting of the chimes that are heard as the curtain descends; and he comes to a certain knowledge of exactly what his cues are. Similarly, the actor learns exactly how many times the telephone is to ring before he is to pick it up, and precisely what is the nature of the chimes to which he must register an emotional reaction at the end of the act. Frequently, these coordinations are worked out and then repeated several times to be certain they are smooth and fixed.

After whatever number of technical rehearsals are required by the complexity of the production, rehearsals should proceed to achieve a sense of complete polish. This stage cannot last too long or the actors may become stale—particularly inexperienced actors. Dress rehearsals are handled precisely as if an audience were present; in late dress rehearsals, it is sometimes profitable to have an audience. When costumes present a particular problem, such as a long train on a dress, the difficult item should be introduced earlier in the rehearsal process. Rehearsals should proceed well past the point of the introduction of distracting technical elements, so that the actors can regain complete integration and polish before the opening performance.

Performance itself may suggest the desirability of additional refinements. A commercial venture may call for drastic revisions in a desperate attempt to salvage something from an obvious quick trip to oblivion. In an artistic sense, however, changes at this point should be slight.

To the production artists, the audience constitutes the very reason for existence. Not only does the audience see the play come to life; it is only before the audience that the actors feel the characters achieve true dimension. The same need for the assembled audience is felt by the playwright. Dramatic art probably imposes the greatest sense of restriction and limitation on the writer of all the literary forms. The German playwright and critic, Lessing, in the eighteenth century, suggested that there was little purpose in going through all that was involved in presenting a play to an audience if the audience received nothing other than what could be obtained as well by staying at home with a good book. In much the same vein, there seems little justification for a writer to accept the limitations of the dramatic form unless he can achieve more than is available to the writer of the novel. The point is that dramatic literature does have its compensating advantages that justify the expenditure of time, energy, and resources on the part of both the production artists—including the playwright—and the members of the audience. These compensations are realized in performance when the impact of the drama, as vivified by production, is intensified by the psychological facilitation of audience members who interact with one another at the very moment of responding to the production.

What motivates an audience to attend the theater? There is no single answer. In all likelihood, the overwhelming majority seek escapism—the opportunity to relax and to forget both the daily routines and the problems looming on the horizon. The theater is not to be scorned for providing such a service. To provide relaxation is to provide something of value; this fact is in no way altered by the realization that some people overdo their attempts to receive this particular benefit. In providing relaxation, the theater must avoid two very real dangers. It must not offer escapism to the exclusion of offering benefits to those who turn to the theater for more substantial fare. It must not do harm in the attempt to do good.

The theater has a great deal to offer beyond escapism. Theater has existed as a religious practice; it can still serve religious purposes. The theater can present philosophical concepts and moral, social, and political issues. The theater can enlarge the audience's understanding of places, people, issues, and points of view. The theater can attack prejudice—not only in its subject matter or its treatment of material, but also in its ability to draw human beings together in a shared emotional experience as they respond as members of the same audience. The theater can arouse sympathy, anger, and ridicule. Satire is a potent weapon available to those who would attack social institutions and practices. Humor and pathos both lend themselves to the building up of sensitivity and sympathy. Tragedy provides a powerful means of exploring the inner nature of man.

When theater lacks ambition to go beyond escapism, what harm can it do in merely attempting to achieve this modest goal? The major difficulty lies in the fact that the rewards for providing an innocuous bit of relaxation are far from modest. The demand for this material is great; so are the rewards. As a result, there is motivation to supply huge quantities of relaxing escapism. The creative process, however, does not lend itself well to mass production. The demand often prompts the adoption of mass-production methods. When this occurs, the playwright derives his material from the theater rather than from life—often unaware of the fact that his sources may also have derived their material from the theater rather than from life. Actors begin to imitate actors. Directors employ familiar techniques rather than seeking to meet the peculiar demands of a unique interpretative task—often led to this by the realization that there is nothing unique to be interpreted. The theater becomes a place of emotional titillation rather than of insight. Plays, like much of our popular music, become more or less novel variations of already familiar elements. Artists work, not creatively but by formula, replacing their artistry with technical dexterity. Although the result is entertaining to many people, and in that sense useful, the insights involved are most commonly distortions. The complexities of actuality are too great to be compressed into a theatrical formula.

There is a subtle and dangerous difference between deriving the occasional benefit of a bit of relaxing escapism and growing up in a culture that is so permeated with escapism as to lead those who respond to it to confuse the distortion with the actuality. A society that has created its governmental institutions on the assumption that an informed citizenry would play an active role in the determination of policy can ill afford to cope with actuality under the influence of a citizenry that is not so much informed as conditioned by imitations of imitations of actuality. It may be maintained that people do not turn to the theater for information. Certainly this is correct. But if theater is viewed as a social phenomenon independent of medium —that is, as including the drama of the film and the television screen as well as of the stage—it must be recognized as a potent force in the development of values.

Clearly, then, the nature of audience response is a matter of considerable significance, socially as well as financially and artistically. Some of the social dimensions have been explored. The financial dimensions are sufficiently obvious. Artistically, two concepts merit some consideration. These are empathy and aesthetic distance—phenomena that are quite meaningfully discussed together. Empathy exists in the theater when the audience identifies with one or more characters. Aesthetic distance is what prevents the identification from going too far; it is the continuous awareness —regardless of the extent to which the production creates an illusion of reality—of the fact that, after all, this is the theater and not life. Of course, theater is exciting just to the extent that it simulates an audience to be "carried away" in the illusion. Nothing but aesthetic distance would be disastrous; empathy is essential. When the audience is indifferent to the events on the stage, too much aware of the unreality of the events to become emotionally involved, the aesthetic distance is too great. When the audience becomes so involved in the action that some its members rush upon the stage to lend physical assistance to one of the characters, the empathy is too great. The desirable balance may be described as establishing as little aesthetic distance as is necessary to prevent too much empathy; or, in reverse terms, to create as much empathy as is possible without completely destroying some sense of aesthetic distance.

Theater as Illusion

In whatever form it is presented, theater is a matter of illusion. Although there are many shadings to each, two basic approaches to the theater exist. These may be labelled *theatricalism* and *actualism*. Both deal in illusion, but in highly different ways.

The illusion of "actualism" is that it *pretends* to deal in actuality. The audience is asked to play a game according to a specific set of rules. Many of the so-called "styles of production," such as fantasy, realism, and naturalism, are simply different sets of rules. The audience comes with a previously established desire to play the game, anxious to learn the specific rules as quickly as possible. The audience is willing and eager to adapt to any variations on the usual set of rules. Everything in this game points toward establishing the illusion that the world which comes to life on the stage is a real world, an "actuality," even though it may not be the same world and the same actuality that exists outside the theater. A variety of styles may be employed from one play to the next. The *realistic* style attempts to give all the elements the superficial appearance of real life. The *naturalistic* style goes as far as it can in the direction of putting on the stage the reality of life rather than merely a superficial copy. *Fantasy* may deal with people and circumstances patently impossible in the world of reality yet internally consistent. Once the audience learns the rules of the fantasy, it goes on from there in a make-believe world to which it reacts with interest and intensity.

Within the framework of the theatrical illusion, the make-believe world exists. The illusion of the fantasy is obvious. Relatively little reflection is necessary to make equally obvious the illusion of the most naturalistic production. The tragic hero does not, in fact, die.

As a modern Russian critic pointed out, complete naturalism will come only with the replacement of the fourth wall. In other words, the naturalistic setting of a living room is not naturalistic, no matter how the furniture is turned, so long as one wall is removed for the benefit of an audience that has assembled to watch and to listen. It follows, of course, that when the fourth wall is replaced, the audience is gone and theater has ceased to exist. The common dimension of "actualism" exists in obvious fantasy, in superficial realism, in a variety of stylizations, and in painstaking attempts at naturalism whenever the production artists seek to create—within a theater —the illusion of action occurring somewhere other than in a theater.

The illusion of "theatricalism" is that it *pretends* to deal quite frankly and openly with theatrical elements. The actors come before the audience as actors. Scenic units that give no impression of being anything other than scenic units are moved into and out of position completely within sight of the audience. No attempt is made to conceal theatrical mechanisms. There is no pressure to maintain consistency to a set of conventions or rules once the premises, however unusual, have been explained and accepted. This approach to theater, however, is also an illusion. It overlooks the basic orientation of the members of the audience who will insist on getting "lost" in an illusion of reality no matter how often they are brought back to a conscious realization of their presence in a theater.

Somewhat comparable to the dependence of complete naturalism on the replacement of the fourth wall, it may be said that complete theatricalism will come only when the actors can be so obvious about their function in the process as to create no illusion of character—in other words, when the actors cease to act. Theater, of course, is as dependent on the actor for existence as on the audience. So long as there are actors who act, there is creation of character. It matters little whether the actor loses his own personal identity in that of a character he brings to life within the framework of a make-believe actuality, or in that of a character he brings to life within the framework of a "theatrical" production. If the man who appears before the audience presents himself as an "actor" with character dimensions other than those of the individual who plays the role of this "actor," acting exists and an illusion is created.

Criticism

The critical function has been discussed already with regard to the enlargement of appreciation and the evaluative distinction among varying levels of excellence, mediocrity, and inferiority. Also considered was the preview function of the reviewer, who is sometimes glorified with the title of "critic." There may be value in devoting some attention to the prime responsibilities of the critic: to the art, to the artists, and to the audience.

What is the theater critic's responsibility to the theater? Basically, it should begin with a profound respect for the theater's capacity to achieve significance and excellence. To be real, such a respect cannot be merely theoretical; it must grow out of the critic's experience of significant and excellent theater. The critic, then, must range far and wide in the past as well as in the present in pursuit of excellence. Having achieved a clear vision of the theater's potential, the critic is equipped to look upon the theater within his immediate scope. What he seeks is to assist that theater to realize its potential. This will call for encouraging certain developments, discouraging trends in some directions, urging patience at times, and occasionally reminding those who labor of the greatness of their capacities. The personality of the critic will affect his methods, and these methods will vary greatly from one excellent critic to the next. But if the criticism is sound, it will seek to serve the needs of the theater—not the critic.

The theater critic's responsibility to the artists of the theater grows out of his realization that only through these artists can theater achieve significance or excellence or even existence. Just as the art must be nourished, so, too, must the artist. This is not to suggest, however, that all who proclaim themselves artists of the theater are, of necessity, what they proclaim. The critic must be prepared to discriminate between the genuine, even in its embryonic state, and the fraudulent. If the interests of the would-be artist conflict with the interests of theater art, the critic must respond to his basic responsibility to the art.

The responsibility of the critic to the audience lies in the critic's awareness of the fact that the audience provides the reason for the theater's existence. The critic must be sensitive to the fact that his role is so integrally related to the theater that criticism, along with the theater as a cultural and artistic entity, must find is justification in its service to the audience. The critic, then, seeks to facilitate the theater's capacity to serve the audience. This is achieved, at times, by enlarging the theater's capacity to provide; it is achieved, at times, by increasing the audience's capacity to receive. Vital to this function is the attempt to develop the ability of the audience to discriminate. The point is to help the audience not to appreciate anything and everything, but to be selective; for only in this way will theater flourish as an art and realize its fullest potential to serve the audience.

The intelligent consumer of criticism does not wish to accept, blindly, whatever the critic says. The intelligent consumer will, rather, evaluate the criticism and decide what to accept and what to reject. In this sense, the consumer functions as a critic of the critic. Such intelligent consumption is facilitated by an understanding of the standards used by the critic. Responsible and effective criticism, therefore, requires a delineation of the standards of the critic.

This delineation is valuable not only for aiding the consumer in evaluating the criticism. There is the added value provided of supplying a basis upon which a perceptive person can, in time, develop his own critical standards. The greatest profit that can come to an individual from criticism is the development of his own capacity to evaluate, to appreciate, to understand. If each person could develop this capacity for himself, there would be no need for people labelled "critics"—not because criticism would become unnecessary, but because criticism would be universal. There is no need for a label to designate those who can read and write in a culture in which everyone is literate, just as there is no need to differentiate those who breathe from those who do not beyond the recognition of life and death.

In the awareness of the desirability of developing a universal critical sense, it becomes apparent that a discussion of criticism is pertinent to everyone who lives in a culture in which theater consumes an appreciable amount of time, energy, and wealth. Of course, despite its desirability, a critical sense will not be developed by everyone—at least, not to any advanced degree. This is because many individuals lack the inclination, many lack the time, and many lack the ability. In this activity, as in every other phase of life, some people will emerge as leaders—as people to whom others will turn, consciously or not, for guidance. The theater and the society in which it functions will be well served if these critical leaders, who are by no means restricted to the ranks of so-called "professional critics," are well equipped to perform their critical task.

What equipment is necessary for the performance of theatrical criticism? The vital ingredients are: a knowledge of the theater—its history, its techniques, its capacities, and its limitations; a respect for the theater; an assumption of the critic's responsibility to the theater, the theater artist, and the audience; and an ability to articulate clearly and understandably the critical response.

CHAPTER V

Theoretical Foundations

The Nature of Theory and
Its Basis in Research

Theory guides practice. Theory is what is known, considered as highly probable, or assumed to be correct. Theory is the truth as people understand it, as they wish to understand it, or as they pretend to understand it. Theory guides practice on these varying bases for highly intelligent men, not merely for the willful or the stupid. A man will base a theory on probability—even on low probability, on assumption, on the nebulous vagueness of personal sensitivity—only if he is ignorant. The most intelligent of men, however, are frequently ignorant. Life often demands practice in areas where knowledge is slight. Whatever guides this practice can be described as theory.

Under the circumstances, it is desirable to base theory as much as possible on certain knowledge or on high probability. To achieve knowledge or to assess degree of probability, careful study is required. Such study is known as *research*. The intelligence with which men can work in any field is dependent on the extent to which the theory that guides their practice is the product of research.

Utilization

The research that provides greater knowledge need not be worked out by each individual who seeks to evolve a theoretical understanding of his field. Were this the case, theory would always remain in a primitive stage of development, limited to the insights and actual knowledge that could be obtained in a single lifetime. Fortunately, it is possible for one research project to pick up where another left off. Fortunately, also, research can profit even those who, for one reason or another, do not undertake to do research themselves. In other words, it is possible for those who have not conducted a research project to utilize the contribution to knowledge made by the research. Whoever would achieve such utilization, however, must know where to go to obtain the report on the research and must be capable of understanding, evaluating, and applying the results of the research.

The major reference sources for research in the field of speech and theater are the publications of the various professional associations. Associations that are particularly active in stimulating research and in publishing journals that report on research of pertinence to people in the field include the Speech Association of America, the American Educational Theater Association, the American Speech and Hearing Association, the National Association of Educational Broadcasters, and the National Society for the Study of Communications. Among the publications of the Speech Association of America is *Speech Monographs,* which publishes lists of graduate theses completed in all areas, as well as lists of research projects under way. Reports on research are presented at conventions of the associations. Much research results in the publishing of scholarly books by university presses or commercial publishing houses. The best way to familiarize oneself with the significant research already done, under way, and being contemplated is through active membership in one or more of the professional associations, attendance at the conventions and conferences, and regular reading of the associations' publications.

Knowing of the existence of a research report, knowing where and how to obtain a copy, even actually having the report in one's possession—none of this is sufficient. The report is of little or no value unless it is understandable. The incomprehensibility of a report frequently results not from any defect in the report itself, but from the inability of the person seeking to read and understand it. Research reporting tends to be compact. For purposes of precision as well as of brevity, the reporter most commonly employs a terminology peculiar to the field. In addition, the investigation may have made use of a technical method, such as statistics, with its own precise and unique terminology. In other words, much research is reported in the form of one specialist presenting material to other specialists. A certain background of knowledge is necessary, therefore, in order to obtain the benefit of the additional knowledge presented in the research report.

It is evident that, if knowledge is necessary to understand a research report, greater knowledge is necessary to evaluate the method of investigation and the value of the results. In speech and theater, during recent years, a progressively greater interest has been manifested in the use of quantitative, experimental, and statistical methods in research. As a result, it has become increasingly necessary for students and scholars in speech and theater to understand these methods. This is true even for the person who has neither the facility nor the desire to utilize these methods himself, but who simply wishes to keep abreast of developments and contributions to knowledge in his field.

The common practice for many people who are unknowledgeable is to assume that what is unintelligible must be profound. Such people read introductions to reports and their conclusions—and accept the conclusions. There are other people who resent their inability to cope with the new techniques and who assume that whatever they find unintelligible is essentially nonsense decked out in impressive terminology. Such people simply refuse to read certain types of reports—and they reject the conclusions.

In many aspects of speech and theater, however, seemingly unreasonable reactions to experimental investigations are not the result of blindness or stubbornness. They reflect, rather, a basic philosophical disagreement as to whether certain dimensions of communicative and aesthetic behavior may be meaningfully subjected to quantified measurement or objective analysis. Whatever merit there may be to the various points of view in any specific instance, speech and theater scholarship has definitely reached the point at which it demands—of any student who would be conversant with the field as a whole—a general working knowledge of a number of research methods, including the experimental. The need for breadth of understanding may be emphasized just as meaningfully for the experimentalist who, in his enthusiasm for a specific investigative method, frequently fails to develop any appreciation of those major research activities that supply the theoretical body of knowledge out of which many of his own experimental hypotheses are derived.

The results of research are applicable to the modification and the development of theory and to the practice that is guided by this theory. Theory must be continuously tested for consistency with the new concepts and insights revealed by research. Research must be continuously tested by the application of its results to practice. Practice is commonly held to be sound to the extent that it is effective. Research methods are utilized to measure effectiveness. Clearly, there is a close, continuous, and mutually beneficial interrelationship among research, theory, and practice. When the interrelationship breaks down, the benefits are not realized. For the interrelationships to exist, communication must be maintained among research scholars, theoreticians, and practitioners. In speech and theater, the inability of specialists to communicate with one another is as much a problem as it is in contemporary society in general. In speech and theater, there are practitioners who work instinctively, theoreticians for whom certain areas of pertinent research are untapped or even inaccessible, and research scholars who are out of touch with the realities of practice.

The best resource for coping with this problem is the university professor who combines within himself (1) the ability and motivation to conduct research, (2) the understanding necessary to benefit from the research of others, (3) the theoretical grasp of the field that is prerequisite to working with students, and (4) either practical skill or, at the least, a close familiarity with the problems and techniques of practical applications. The last is necessary because of his task, as a teacher, to develop the ability of others to practice effectively. Needless to say, these elements are not combined in every university professor. Factors have been at work in speech and theater, as in other academic disciplines, to discourage rather than to foster such combinations. One of these factors is the demand for teachers that has become so insistent as to result in the acceptance of teachers who are poorly equipped or inadequately motivated to do research. Another such factor is the tendency, usually encouraged by the research scholar himself, to divorce the research function from the teaching function. Whatever seems best or whatever directions are taken, those who work in speech and theater must remain sensitive to the problem and seek the means of coping with it, at least for themselves.

Research Purposes

Research in speech and theater normally has one or more of three types of objectives: reconstruction, analysis, and prediction. In a very rough sense, it is possible to discriminate here on the basis of the direction of view. *Reconstruction* deals with the past; *analysis,* with what exists in the present; *prediction,* with the future.

There are many advantages to be derived from an understanding of the past. A knowledge of the theater for which Shakespeare wrote—its physical structure, the composition of its audience, its production methods—enlarges one's appreciation of Shakespeare's writing techniques and contributes to the effectiveness of a contemporary production of Shakespeare's plays. A knowledge of the speaking situation of Lincoln's First Inaugural Address—the place of delivery, the problems of the country, the fears in people's minds —enlarges one's appreciation of what Lincoln said and how he said it and contributes to the effectiveness of a contemporary analysis of his speaking. A knowledge of the production methods of the ancient Chinese theater may provide an idea for solving a contemporary production problem. A knowledge of past methods employed in the treatment of a specific speech defect may facilitate the search for a better method. In general, a knowledge of the past provides the opportunity to build on what has been accomplished rather than starting all over again; it extends the area in which the search for excellence can be conducted rather than forcing standards of evaluation that are based on too limited a perspective.

Analysis is a detailed examination of material presently available. Material may be presently available because it has just recently come into existence; or it may be available because it has been reconstructed out of the past. Whether the speech text or the play script is contemporary or historical in date of origin, the text or script must be existent in the present in order to be subjected to analysis. Detailed examination is not limited to objects as tangible as written documents. It is possible to analyze the results of a therapeutic technique, the emotional reactions of an audience, shifts in attitude as a result of a persuasive speech, and prevailing policies of broadcast station managers with regard to qualification requirements for new personnel. It is possible, too, to conduct a detailed examination in areas where very precise measurements can be made—to analyze the technical facilities of a specific theater, the certification requirements for speech therapists in the school systems of various states and regions of the country, and the percentage of time devoted to different types of programming in the broadcast operation of a particular radio or television station during a given period.

Many decisions—perhaps most of them—must be made in situations in which there is much uncertainty. The precise facts are not always known. When this is the case, the action taken is the one that gives the greatest promise of success. The decision as to which action seems most likely to result in success is a decision with regard to the future; it involves prediction under conditions of uncertainty. Such decisions are unavoidable; no action at all is, in itself, a course of action and the result of a decision—however unconsciously or reluctantly made. Prediction is inherent in speech and theater activity. The play director is constantly making decisions regarding the response of an audience to what is being prepared in rehearsal. The persuasive speaker decides between humor and seriousness, between climactic or anticlimactic order in the presentation of his main arguments, and what part of the presentation will be most appropriate for making his persuasive intent clear to the audience—all on the basis of believing himself capable of making some predictions regarding the future behavior of his audience. Decisions as to the use of a hearing aid or a particular therapeutic technique in coping with a hearing loss or an articulatory defect are essentially predictive decisions.

The Research Problem

The research problem grows out of practical or theoretical needs. The problem of a research worker in speech or theater is pertinent to other workers in speech and theater just because of its origin in the very work which these people are doing. The pertinence is not always obvious, however. The layman is inclined to inquire, at times, as to the practical value of a particular research project. This is true with regard to speech and theater research as with many other fields. The reason for this is that those who are specialists rather than laymen have a theoretical as well as a practical interest. The practical value of the testing of theoretical hypotheses is not immediately apparent; it is, nonetheless, of vital importance.

The research scholar is concerned not only with the pertinence or significance of the problem that he feels a need to explore; he is also desirous of knowing about all previous explorations of this or any related problem. This is not simply a matter of determining whether someone has or has not already conducted an investigation. If there is still a need for exploration, the investigator should profit as much as possible from the explorations of others. On rare occasions, a previous research project in the same area may have been poorly done. Not uncommonly, additional materials have been brought to light since the earlier investigation was conducted, or refined methods have been developed that permit a more detailed or precise type of investigation to be undertaken. Most often, the problem itself has many complexities, and previous investigations have been able to explore only a limited number of aspects. The most fruitful results will be obtained, therefore, from an investigation that is carefully articulated with other investigations in the area.

On the basis of the felt need for practical or theoretical knowledge, an awareness of the attempts already made to satisfy this need, and a concept of the significance of probing one or another aspect of the problem suggested by the need, the investigator can arrive at a rough definition of the research problem upon which he wishes to concentrate. At this point he must inquire into the resources available to him for conducting the research. This check includes such items as library materials, laboratory equipment, measurement techniques, time, personnel, financial support, computing facilities, and his own personal knowledge of and ability in research methodology. The nature of the resources may impose many limitations on the study. In light of the resources and the limitations, the problem is redefined and cast in concrete and specific terms.

To exemplify all this, a hypothetical problem can be considered. A teacher of playwriting and the theory of dramaturgy may feel a need to formulate somewhat more precisely his concepts of the techniques employed by playwrights to establish the details of characterization. This need grows out of a working situation in which he finds himself informing creative writers of the techniques available to them for developing characterization in their dramatic writing. He knows that this is a matter of significance because he knows how important it is to the creative writer to master the techniques of his medium. A careful study of the literature on this subject may reveal a considerable amount of theoretical discussion but no objective study of techniques actually employed by practicing playwrights. The investigator may then roughly define his research problem as an objective analysis of the characterizing devices actually employed by practicing playwrights.

Such an objective analysis must be limited in some way, even if the investigator is prepared to devote a lifetime to the investigation; and it is quite likely that the significance of the problem would not justify such an expenditure of time for any investigator. Just to consider this limitation, therefore, the research study might be limited to the American theater, and further limited to the period of 1920–1945, still further limited to the most successful playwrights of this period, and finally limited to the most successful serious plays of these playwrights. Standards of selection, of course, would have to be established. Redefinition of the research problem, then, might result in considering it as an objective analysis of the characterizing techniques employed in the most successful serious plays written by the most successful playwrights in the American theater during the period 1920–1945.

Research Methods

Research methods of investigation are selected in the same way in which woodworking tools are selected—that is, on the basis of the task to be performed. The research methods, then, may be reconstructive, analytic, or predictive, to serve the purposes of reconstruction, analysis, and prediction. Research methods used in speech and theater are commonly described as *historical, descriptive,* and *experimental.* These latter terms are so widely employed that they should be part of any student's vocabulary and they should be understood in their interrelationships with respect to the basic purposes.

The reconstructive method pieces together the clues that can be discovered in determining something of the past. Both the discovery techniques and the piecing-together procedures are integral parts of the method. To the extent that an historical study discovers clues and pieces them together, such a study employs the reconstructive method. Because the historical study always does employ this method, the method is generally termed historical. It will be valuable to have a more precise understanding, however, since historical studies frequently attempt more than this. For example, a rhetorical study of a significant speaker of the past is considered to be historical. Certainly, such a study reconstructs the past. Much of the purpose of this reconstruction, however, is to bring to light— and to understand in relation to what has been reconstructed— manuscripts of public addresses made by that significant speaker. These manuscripts are not merely presented; they are carefully analyzed. The application of the techniques required to make this analysis constitutes a major part of the rhetorical study; these techniques, however, are not part of the reconstructive method.

The analytic method examines in detail and describes. Many studies employing the analytic method are labelled descriptive studies and considered to be using the descriptive method. The descriptive method label is commonly reserved, however, for those analytic methods employed in studies that are neither historical nor experimental, despite the fact that both historical and experimental studies may employ analytic methods of investigation. Reference has just been made to the employment of the analytic method in a type of historical study. An example of the use of this method in an experimental study will be considered shortly. Examples of the analytic method in a study that is neither historical nor experimental would be: (1) the use of a questionnaire to determine the attitudes of former debaters regarding the significance or nonsignificance of their debate experience; (2) a survey of the way the basic course in public speaking is taught throughout the colleges and universities of the United States; and (3) a study of the working methods of a particular director in the contemporary theater.

The predictive method seeks to establish patterns of interrelationship that will indicate, given specific elements, what the outcome is likely to be. Experience provides an excellent means of arriving at concepts of such patterns. In a conscious, methodological sense, however, this end is usually sought through experimentation. Much experimentation is of a trial-and-error sort and involves measurements that are highly subjective. Experimentation can be much more refined, however, employing precise, objective measurement within carefully controlled situations and sophisticated statistical tests to determine the significance of measured differences. This more refined experimentation is what is commonly described by most references to an experimental study employing an experimental method. An example of this would be an attempt to measure the relative effectiveness of different utilizations of television in a teaching-learning situation. A study undertaking to measure relative effectiveness is essentially predictive in nature, probing the question of which teaching method will result in the most learning.

Such a study could be conducted by carefully controlled experimentation; it could also be carried out by a subjective comparison, on the teacher's part, of the relative merits of different procedures tried at different times, with different students, with no careful control of variables. Although the latter approach may seem rather unscientific, it is undoubtedly the basis upon which most teachers develop most of their refinements in teaching theory and practice. When an educational system expresses a preference for experienced teachers, it assumes that teachers learn from experience that is, for the most part, trial-and-error experimentation. The point is, however, that the ability to draw conclusions from either type of experimentation—carefully controlled or crude trial and error—depends on the results of measurement of student learning. Such measurement, in turn—however subjective or objective—is based on an analysis of course content. Analysis, in other words, is an integral part of such an experimental study.

In summary, it is possible to say that research studies are meaningfully classified as historical, descriptive, and experimental. The methods employed in these studies commonly take their name from the name of the study. This usage is so common that anyone who would do research or make use of research would profit from understanding what is meant by the historical, descriptive, and experimental methods. In actuality, however, such studies frequently employ more than one method. A fuller understanding may be achieved, therefore, by thinking of the way in which reconstructive, analytic, and predictive methods are adapted to the needs of historical, descriptive, and experimental research.

Theoretical Orientations

Those who conduct research and those who would benefit from it find themselves involved, in many instances, in basic conflicts of theoretical orientation with regard to problems, methods, and significance. There is value in considering at least some representative examples of such conflicts. In doing so, care must be taken to re-member that the conflicts are of orientation, not of evidence or fact.

Communication theory provides divergent emphases on linguistic structure, semantic significance, and organizational channels. A linguistic orientation results in a research focus on the form of the communication. A semantic orientation results in a focus on the psychological motivations, responses, and interactions of those in-volved in the communication. An organizational orientation results in a focus on the channels of communication.

In rhetoric there is a marked divergence of method. The old tra-dition of classical rhetoric occupies an honored position that many consider to be the soundest and most fruitful basis for rhetorical scholarship. Some rhetoricians start from the same base but con-sider it necessary to devise new frameworks and new terminologies. There are also those who believe that the real key to significant insights is the use of precise and carefully controlled experimental procedures. Some rhetoricians take all persuasive communication as their sphere; others limit themselves to speech.

Speech communication is examined from the standpoint of the techniques of the speaker—with adaptation to the audience being one part of the process of speaking—or from the standpoint of a group relationship. The emphasis in one case is on the individual seeking to achieve an objective through speech. The emphasis in the other case is on the speech process through which a group progresses toward the formulation—consciously articulated or not —and achievement of an objective.

Theater scholars exhibit a variety of interests. Some devote all their energies to historical reconstruction. There have been limited applications of controlled experimental methods in recent years in the area of audience-response patterns. Some attention has been given to analyzing the techniques and aesthetic philosophies of working artists.

In the area of oral interpretation, there is an increasing emphasis on literary analysis. This has grown to the point where some schol-ars feel that the distinction between interpretative and literary anal-ysis is, in essence, nonexistent. Interpretative analysis focuses on the techniques of interpreting literature through speech. Such anal-ysis depends on the analysis necessary to understand the literature. Interpretative analysis, however, demands a concentration on techniques of speech delivery. To those who fear that such a concentration will result in a mechanical and highly artificial approach to interpretation, it seems desirable to assume that the interpreter will be an expressive and sensitive speaker and that, as a scholar, his efforts should be restricted to literary analysis. To those who accept mechanics and artifice as basic ingredients in any art, there is a desire to come to grips with the techniques of delivery as elements to be studied and mastered on the assumption that their mastery can be sufficient to result in so expressive a delivery that the techniques are not apparent. In addition to this concern with analysis—literary or interpretative—there is, also, a concern with historical background and a concern with audience response. Relatively little has been done in applying experimental methods to interpretation techniques—at least by scholars in the field of interpretation—because of the contemporary emphasis on the techniques of literature rather than the techniques of interpretation.

Radio and television are employed in a variety of ways. Research has been done in the way that broadcasting functions in society, both in the United States and in other countries. Much research has been done in the educational uses of radio and television. Research in the technical aspects is a matter of concern to the electronics engineer; it is pertinent to the student of speech and theater only as it affects the method or content of production or the impact of the media on society.

The resources of modern scientific developments have been employed most consciously and effectively, in speech research, in the areas of speech science, pathology, and audiology. Within these areas may be found investigators with different emphases. Some function primarily as physical scientists, others as medical scientists, and others as psychologists, while still others combine different approaches in varying degrees.

A great deal of research in speech and theater concerns itself with educational methodology. This applies both to the methods of teaching speech and theater and to the methods of utilizing speech and theater in teaching. In both areas there are divergent attitudes with regard to the use of controlled experimentation. Some investigators insist that such experimentation is the only approach to objectivity. Other investigators contend that the process of controlling variables distorts the matters being investigated so as to make the results, however significant in the experimental situation, inapplicable to actuality.

Contemporary Challenges

The need for expanded knowledge to enlarge the theory that guides speech and theater practice presents a challenge to all involved in speech and theater activity. Those involved should realize the nature of the challenge and their own potential for responding.

The practicing teacher can make two major contributions. The teacher can test theory. The teacher can be sensitive to the need for specific information—as this need is made apparent in the practice of those who are applying the theory or seeking to understand it.

The individual theoretician can contribute the formulation of research problems that grow out of his search for a theory that is sufficiently inclusive and consistent. The theoretician can engage in a continuous process of seeking to integrate all knowledge brought to light by investigation. This process of integration frequently demands the alteration of theoretical concepts.

Organizations have profound contribution potentials. This includes educational institutions, professional associations, research and philanthropic foundations, and government agencies. Such organizations have objectives that can be served, frequently, by speech and theater research. The responsibility to recognize the specific areas of service is, theoretically, a shared responsibility. In a practical sense, the responsibility rests on the research scholar in speech and theater, who must be sensitive to a number of factors. First, it should be clear that organizational support is dependent on energy expended to seek such support. Second, organizational support is justified only to the extent that the projects supported contribute to the objectives of the organization. Third, organizational support is not an objective but a means to an end and must be viewed as such by the investigator as well as by the organization. That is, organizational support should not be sought or cherished for its own sake; whatever prestige or activity it creates, it is essentially unproductive to the speech or theater scholar—as such—unless it contributes significantly to the knowledge, theory, or practice of those in the fields of speech and theater.

CHAPTER VI

Speech Education: Conventional
Forms and Principles

Relation of Theory to Practice

The basis of improvement in speech is the application of sound and appropriate theory to intelligently directed practice in the most useful speech forms. Having treated the concepts of general theory in earlier chapters, let us turn to a consideration of what constitutes the useful forms. The point of beginning is found in the nature of speech and the circumstances by which the child learns and practices speech, namely, the demands of his daily life. There he is not concerned with theory but only with results; and his understandings, standards, and goals may be accidental rather than the result of deliberate or wise choices. The implications for his progress need no exposition. There is, however, a body of theory concerning speech and its improvement that has been developed and tested. It derives from the observation and analysis of man's use of speech in his functional activities, from experimentation and practice in teaching-learning situations, and from research with new approaches to speech improvement. The guidelines which emerge clearly indicate that this theory should be applied to specific goals or objectives, namely: (1) understanding the elements of the speech act; (2) identifying specific problems to be solved by the individual; (3) understanding the relative importance of ideas, attitudes, and feelings in the speech process; and (4) establishing clear, limited, and reasonable goals for personal improvement.

Two principles should guide effective practice in the various speech forms. First, speech should be purposive with respect to securing appropriate, specific, and limited audience response, while contributing to individual improvement by the speaker. Second, the practice should be varied and inclusive, so that the individual gains skill in handling the most common and useful forms. As men go about their daily lives, they find a need to communicate for the purpose of exchanging information, solving problems cooperatively, attempting to influence belief or action, sharing experiences and feelings, and seeking to facilitate social relationships. Out of the activity to meet these needs emerge conventional speech forms that we use frequently, informally, and often unconsciously. The quality of our performance may range from poor to good; improvement requires the identification of these forms plus knowledge of their nature and potential.

Conversational Speech

Informal or conversational speech is the most universal and important means of oral communication. A specific definition is difficult, since a variety of activities falls within this class. Such speech may range from various kinds of casual and social conversation to purposive telephoning, interviewing, and committee work. Under certain conditions, these may merge gradually into more formal types of expression where an individual in conversation may be the center of the group's attention and may find himself presenting a semiformal public speech. A semiformal committee meeting may turn into an informal discussion and in the end become more formalized, perhaps making use of parliamentary procedure and legislative debate. The distinctions are clear at the extremes, but there is a middle area where exact definition is neither necessary nor desirable and where its absence in no way affects the understanding or application of the principles involved. Neither does such lack of specific delineation reduce the importance of informal speech to the individual and to society. Undoubtedly, it is the most frequently used and significant vehicle for the transaction of the essential business of human society.

This type of speech is constantly being taught in schools. The point is that it is often taught only incidentally and should be taught more effectively. Our basic body of theory applies fully and productively in all respects. Appropriate content and student activities exist at all levels.

The teaching of this speech form and the evaluation of results are challenging tasks for the teacher. Some of the instruction will be direct and specific, but a major portion of the teaching and almost all of the application will, of necessity, be indirect. Involved are highly personal reactions and complex relationships. Student progress may appear to be irregular or slow. Conventional techniques of evaluation may prove inadequate, and in many cases intermediary persons and highly subjective judgments may be involved. Despite all these difficulties, experience and observation have demonstrated that significant positive results are possible.

Public Speaking

As the informal communicative situation becomes less fluid and takes on more specific patterns and characteristics, we refer to it as public speaking. Such speech is one of the most common forms of student communication in the American school and occupies a place of equal importance in our adult life. It is so widely used in such a variety of circumstances that a broad definition is necessary. A working description would classify public speaking as a single individual talking to a group of listeners by means of relatively continuous discourse, in an attempt to achieve a specific end that has been chosen by the speaker. This definition embodies the three generally recognized characteristics of public speech, namely: (1) a single speaker addressing a group of listeners; (2) the speaker's effort to modify audience knowledge, belief, or action; and (3) a relatively uninterrupted focus on the speaker as the source of stimulation.

Many people engage in public speaking without consciously identifying the activity. While it is common for persons to express concern when required to present a speech labeled as "public," this is often a matter of perception and association. Acutely aware of, and often overly sensitive to, a focus of attention on themselves, they feel a sense of psychological isolation resulting in insecurity and discomfort. But the same individuals will feel at ease and communicate more adequately when presenting a report, explaining a problem, making a request, giving directions, recounting an experience, or supporting a belief in situations that meet all the tests of a public speech but do not happen to be so labeled or perceived. Specific examples of this abound. Students in school report on topics in social studies, present book reports in English, explain problems in mathematics and science, address their peers in clubs and student-governing groups, and engage in public meetings. All these are semiformal or formal public speeches. Such opportunities should and could be expanded and extended to include all students. Their values to the individual and to the group are unquestioned. One of the limitations, however, is the lack of student training and experience in handling such communication easily and productively.

Public speaking finds one of its most important uses in the deliberative activities of men. The primary form is exposition, where the purpose is to provide information that is clear, accurate, meaningful, and useful to the listener. More specific purpose must always be cast in terms of the interrelationships of subject, audience, situation, and speaker. There is no major form of cooperative human endeavor that does not call for expository speaking. Wherever people need to learn about new ideas, relationships, developments, processes, potentials, implications, or activities, such speaking may be necessary. Examples from education have been cited already. Additional illustrations are found in supervisors explaining work arrangements, teachers presenting a program of study to colleagues or parents, a union member explaining the working conditions in a particular shop, representatives of a civic committee discussing a proposed bond issue or zoning law, a scientist pointing out potentials of space exploration, and a student discussing the values of a foreign student exchange program.

The most obvious characteristics of such speaking are objectivity of treatment, direct disclosure of purpose, clear organization, supporting material geared to audience interest and needs, simple and understandable language—especially when presenting new or complex material—frequent summaries, delivery that is direct, restrained, and adapted to the audience, and limited use of emotional appeals. Such speaking represents, in fact, the means by which information is acquired and related and is, therefore, the foundation for potential action on the part of the listener.

A second major form of deliberative public speech is termed persuasion. This also is used with great frequency and is present, to some degree, in most deliberations. The fundamental purpose is to so impress and arouse the listeners that they accept and eventually act in accordance with the speaker's proposals or desires. To achieve this purpose, the persuasive speaker adapts himself to the motivations of his listeners. The effective persuader, therefore, must have extensive knowledge of both his subject and his audience, as well as great skill in developing appeals, particularly when dealing with apathetic or hostile listeners.

Misunderstanding of the nature of persuasion, coupled with examples of its unethical application, have caused many people to regard it as inherently evil and as employing methods to be scrupulously avoided. Viewed objectively, persuasion *per se* is neither good nor bad. Actually, it is a part of our daily life from which we cannot and should not isolate ourselves. We find it present in most public speech. We customarily think of it associated with salesmanship or political campaigns, but it also exists in appeals to support youth programs, the request to purchase tickets for a worthy cause, the Sunday morning sermon, and the arguments concerning a resolution before a professional meeting. Many persuasive appeals are implied, if not directly stated, in speeches that appear to be principally expository. Most speakers find a need to learn how to employ persuasion, and all listeners must be prepared to recognize, analyze, and evaluate such appeals as a means of self-protection.

The unique characteristics of persuasive speech include selectivity and subjectivity in treatment of content, the possible withholding of the speaker's purpose until favorable attention and interest have been aroused, and an organization intended to secure the desired reaction from the particular audience addressed. In addition, supporting material should be vivid, appealing, and dynamic—integrating emotional and logical appeals. Persuasion employs language that is vivid and sometimes repetitive and rhythmical. The delivery should reflect the intensity of the speaker's feelings without suggesting lack of control, and the entire presentation should culminate in arousing the listener to accept the belief or engage in the action that the speaker desires.

Paralleling deliberative speech are the ceremonial forms intended to commemorate, recall, or revive feelings and memories, facilitate social relationships, serve symbolic purposes, or observe the demands of courtesy and ritual. Intended to reaffirm or reassure rather than to present new ideas or call for unusual action, such speaking generally follows familiar formats. Ceremonial speaking has been a part of man's social activity through all history, and its importance has not diminished in contemporary society. Typical situations where such forms are employed are welcomes, presentations, tributes, introductions, dedications, anniversaries, speeches to entertain, eulogies, and the like. Their importance is self-evident. While they occasionally take on a deliberative turn the vast majority do not deviate from the conventional patterns.

Some of the characteristics of this form are in direct contrast to those of expository or persuasive speech. Of great importance are adaptation to the particular situation and simplicity of purpose, which, along with the manner of content development, place minimum demands on the audience members. Such speaking must have high audience appeal and make use of colorful, courteous, and sometimes elevated language without seeming to be extravagant or inappropriate. Emotional appeals are generally clear, simple, and directed to the more altruistic sentiments. Warmth and enthusiasm should be reflected in a dynamic presentation.

Whatever the degree of formality or the range of complexity, both practice and instruction in speech must be considered as a total, complex, integrated action. Thus, it is meaningful to point out that the concepts and principles which follow are common to all forms of public address and should be related appropriately not only to the forms of individual speaking that have preceded this discussion but also to the group forms of discussion and debate which follow. They also have application in radio and television speech.

The speaker is faced with certain tasks or obligations: (1) the discovery or generation of ideas and methods of treating material; (2) the arrangement of materials; (3) the selection of language; (4) the presentation or delivery—involving both voice and bodily action; and (5) the memorization of the material (an element given greater importance in classical rhetoric than in contemporary practice). In addition, the speaker's relationship to the audience creates ethical considerations to which both parties must be sensitive. As he selects and arranges subject matter, the speaker must be concerned with the truth, the worth, and the justification of his ideas. He will need to ask himself such questions as:

1. Do I know that what I speak is true?
2. Do I respect fully the integrity of the listener and present my ideas so as to reflect that attitude?
3. Do I withhold any material that the listener should know if he is to judge my proposals intelligently?

4. Do I have full intellectual and logical support for my message as well as appropriate and effective emotional appeals?
5. Do I place my personal interest in conflict with public welfare?
6. Do I use feedback objectively and constructively to reappraise the content of my speech and to modify its presentation?

The burden is not the speaker's alone, however. The listener has a manifold obligation. He should extend to the speaker the same consideration which he expects from the speaker. He should strive to listen carefully and objectively, withholding judgment until he has heard the speaker out. For his own welfare as well as that of others, he should expect and demand ethical speech behavior from those who address him. He must be alert to discover, as well as to make appropriate adjustments and compensations for, such inadequacies.

In all forms of public address, knowledge about and belief in a worthwhile subject are of primary importance. In these elements is found the major source of confidence, motivation, and capacity for total response on the part of the speaker. In addition, such qualities help insure that audiences will receive interesting and valuable ideas; the speaker should be capable of delivering such intellectual goods. Mastery of content is essential, but will not in itself insure effective speech. Given a worthy subject, the speaker's purpose should be clear, specific, appropriate, and possible of accomplishment. The speaker must know what he wishes to achieve in addressing a particular audience and must subject all aspects of preparation and delivery to the test of contributing to this achievement. The general ends of public speaking are to interest (sometimes modified to include to entertain), to inform, to impress, or to persuade. Within these broad areas, specific audience reactions must be selected and preparation must be governed accordingly.

As a speaker attempts to formulate and present his message, he must decide how to employ and balance logical, emotional, and ethical appeals. Logical appeals are intellectual in nature, employing both information (evidence) and relationship (reason). These are necessary to test ideas and propositions, and neither speaker nor listener can ignore them, except at their own peril. Most individuals allege that they hold logic in high regard, desire speakers to use it, employ it themselves, and are guided by it. In reality, it has been established repeatedly—and the disastrous results often noted —that most people reason poorly and disregard the sound logic of others. This is not to suggest that we should discontinue our efforts to employ reason more effectively.

In contrast, emotional appeals are directed primarily to the feelings, sentiments, and desires of the listeners. Such appeals are a necessary part of any speech intended to move listeners to a response that has depth and intensity. Most people are readily affected by such appeals and, in employing them, the speaker should himself be capable of experiencing in suitable degree the emotion he seeks to evoke. In evoking emotions, the speaker finds that concrete, specific, and pictorial materials are more effective than general or abstract appeals. Whatever emotional appeals are employed, they should be tested consistently and carefully against logical and ethical standards. Most effective speeches employ a judicious combination of emotion and logic for mutual reinforcement. Such speeches produce the more lasting results.

A third type of appeal arises from the audience's perception of the speaker and is termed his ethos, or "ethical appeal." (This should not be confused with the ethical standards adopted by the speaker.) Whenever a speaker comes before an audience, such impressions are always operative. It behooves the speaker to do all that is possible to insure that his ethos is positive or favorable. Aristotle tells us that factors contributing to ethos are evidences available to the audience which indicate the speaker's intelligence, good character, and good will. Modern communication has not changed these basic elements, but has added another. Now it is possible for certain information about the speaker's reputation and personality to precede his appearance. Such elements are now added factors in audience perception and reaction. A speaker's ethos appears to be most effective when the audience perceives what Quintillian described as "a good man skilled in speech." Such impressions may generally be enhanced by honesty, integrity, and good will in both private and public life, evidence of diligent application and sincere conviction, warmth of personality, and concern for the interests of others.

Discussion and Debate

Against this background let us consider two forms of public address—discussion and debate—that involve groups of speakers rather than a single individual. Discussion is one of our oldest and most useful types of speech. We may describe it as a cooperative deliberation of problems by people who think and converse together in face-to-face or co-acting groups to arrive at a common understanding or action. This form involves something more than the casual or social conversations that were considered under informal speech. As here conceived, discussion may range from informal to highly organized public deliberations. It is a deliberate, purposive method by which men exchange information, consider problems and policies, and explore possibilities of agreement. Along with debate, it represents one of the tools of our free society.

Fundamentally, discussion is a problem-solving activity; it is facilitated when the substance for discussion is phrased in the form of a question. There is little point in discussing questions of fact; greatest profit derives from considering those of value or policy. Discussion is basically cooperative and democratic in nature, employing reflective or constructive thinking as contrasted with intentional thinking. One approach to discussion may be described as the attempt to apply the scientific method of inquiry to the solution of personal or social problems. It is well described as thought in process.

Customarily, discussion is used in two forms. When relatively small face-to-face groups—ranging in number from three to about twenty—meet to discuss, we term this informal or round-table discussion. An extensive body of literature has resulted from the efforts of students in speech, psychology, and sociology to study the nature and functioning of such groups. In general, they can be said to have the following qualities or characteristics:

1. A common problem is recognized and defined.
2. There is a commitment on the part of members to the concept of discussion and an acceptance of the attitudes and procedures necessary to carry on the process.
3. The group establishes its own realistic goals, at the same time making possible an accommodation of personal needs and goals.
4. There exists an equality of relationship among the group members

involving such things as participation, contribution to group work, and responsibility for the final product; and all this results in much spontaneous interaction among members of the group.

5. There exists within the group a capacity and willingness to engage in critical, objective analysis of the problem at hand.
6. The group recognizes its own resources and is willing to use these productively.
7. There is a willingness to accept the concept of democratic leadership as it develops within the group, and a recognition of its importance in satisfying group needs.
8. There is recognition and acceptance of the fact that the process may involve digressions, delays, and apparent inefficiency as a part of the creative group work.
9. The group accepts possible provisions for utilizing resource persons in the areas of either substance or process.

Situations in which informal discussion has actual or potential use are many and varied. Although seldom formalized, discussion is one of the basic patterns of communication in the family when any group consideration of problems is involved. Voluntary civic and religious organizations employ it widely. In one form or another, it is used in interviewing and counseling—including vocational, financial, and personal guidance work. Business, military, and political personnel spend much time in both informal and formal conferences; and discussion is an indispensable part of governmental operation in both the administrative and the legislative areas. Education employs it at all levels and in all phases of activity ranging from formal instruction through the deliberations of professional committees and administrative conferences to the conduct of association programs.

The values of discussion are self-evident and are reflected in personal development and satisfaction, as well as in organizational efficiency and progress. Discussion is a method of learning that provides freedom to explore ideas, to draw from the thinking and experience of others, and to synthesize the contributions in a constructive manner. As noted earlier, it is a basic tool of democracy, permitting the pooling of resources, objective adaptation, and group unity. At the same time, it is the means by which we may become more sensitive to, and skillful in, human relations. Certainly discussion is one of the best methods for solving certain types of problems, particularly where fixed guidelines may not be available and where social utility and acceptability may be a primary consideration. Successful discussion teaches and requires cooperation and provides a means for handling controversy objectively and constructively.

The second form, public discussion, applies many of the same principles and procedures to larger and more formal groups. In general, the audience observes and participates to a limited degree while chosen individuals carry on the discussion process in a manner adapted to the particular audience or problem. An effort is made to retain all the characteristics and procedural aspects present in informal discussion except as they are modified by the need for definite structure and orderly procedure. Participation is directed and digressions are minimized. The principal discussants or participants are frequently chosen because of known differences in point of view or because of their ability to function well before an audience. On some occasions, they may be chosen because of their particular position or prestige rather than for their substantive competence. Whenever differences in point of view are the primary criteria for choice, there is danger that discussion may merge into debate.

Other modifications involve physical arrangements that allow the audience to see and hear easily. The role of the chairman frequently becomes specialized, and he may be limited to serving as presiding individual rather than becoming involved in the substantive aspects. Frequently there is a forum period following the discussion by the principals. Then the audience may ask questions or perhaps express personal points of view. This often provides general involvement and stimulation, leading to heightened interest.

A wide variety of activities may be classified as public discussion; the most common forms are the panel, the symposium, and the lecture-forum. In the panel, several persons under the direction of a leader discuss a problem among themselves. They are, however, seen and heard by an audience and they are fully aware that the discussion is being carried on primarily for the benefit of the audience rather than for themselves. In a symposium, several individuals in turn make short presentations considering some aspect or position of a problem. These speeches are generally from five to ten minutes in length; at their conclusion, the principals may discuss among themselves or there may be a forum period in which the audience participates. In the lecture-forum, one individual presents an analysis of a problem or his own position with respect to it. This usually requires a minimum of twenty minutes; at the conclusion of his speech either a selected panel, the audience, or both, raise questions and present statements or points of view. It is obvious that these basic forms may be subject to all manner of variations, ranging from dialogues to committee hearings and lecture-panel-forums. The possibilities are limited only by the nature of the problems to be considered, the purposes to be served, and the provision for audience members.

Debate is the counterpart of discussion. Where the former stresses cooperation, the latter emphasizes advocacy. Debate may be defined as competitive oral discourse among two or more advocates who are committed to logically incompatible positions on a specific proposition. Ideally, discussion should precede debate, and the latter should be employed only when the individuals have found it impossible to agree on a particular solution to a problem. Lack of understanding of the nature of these two forms may result in their inappropriate use. Two questions that should always be asked are, "Have we exhausted the possibilities of discussion?" and "Should we begin to debate?" People frequently allege that debate leads to contentiousness, unpleasantness, and hostility. Actually, everyone employs the methods of debate in a great number of situations—whether these be informal or formal, public or private. It is the method of rigorous and analytical comparison and the procedure by which we decide or formalize policy in democratic societies.

An examination of the characteristics of debate will indicate not only its nature but the manner in which it differs from discussion. The parties to a debate have ceased to search for a point of view or a solution to a problem. They believe they have found the most desirable position on the issue and they are attempting to secure general acceptance of that point of view. Propositions for debate, whether stated or implied, are usually concerned with matters of value or policy—although, in certain circumstances, questions of fact may be considered. These propostions are stated in a simple sentence that proposes a change from existing conditions. The reasoning of both parties is intentional rather than reflective. Where a confrontation of speakers takes place, there are generally stated or understood rules governing the order of speaking, the time limits to be observed, and similar factors. The ultimate objective of debate is a decision, a vote, or an action favoring one side or position and rejecting the other. Such a vote or action may come immediately following the debate, or it may be postponed to a later time—but the gaining of a favorable decision is the objective of each party.

When used as an educational method, debate may be conducted under somewhat specialized rules and arrangements. The principal purpose is to train students in the analysis of problems, the development of clear and logical arguments, and the effective support and defense of a point of view. Subjects considered are usually public issues and the emphasis is on evidence, reasoning, and refutation. Decisions, criticisms, and evalutions are generally provided. The purpose here, however, is a vote not on the merits of the issue itself but rather on the quality of debating demonstrated by the student participants.

Educational debate most commonly involves two teams of two persons each. The affirmative has the burden of proposing a change as provided by the agreed-upon proposition. The negative is obliged to defend the *status quo* or support an alternative significantly different from the position taken by the affirmative. Each debater presents what is termed a "principal" or "main" speech, usually of eight to twelve minutes in length, and an additional rebuttal speech, usually four to six minutes in length. It is customary for the affirmative to open the debate. The teams present their main speeches in alternate order. The negative then opens the rebuttal and again the sides alternate. Each speaker, then, gives one main speech and one rebuttal speech, with the alternations so arranged that the affirmative opens the debate and has the final rebuttal. Variations of this form include cross-questioning and providing for a forum period in which additional people may participate. These and other variations are described in detail in most conventional textbooks in the field. Regardless of the modifications, the basic format remains: the affirmative has the burden of proof for proposing a change, it is entitled to open and close the debate, and equal time is allocated to each side.

The importance of discussion and debate in both course and co-curricular work has been recognized, and the development of both forms has been encouraged by the National University Extension Association's Committee on Debate and Discussion Materials. The national office is located at the University of Oregon in Eugene. It has two principal functions. Each year it provides the administrative machinery by which the high schools of the nation select the national problem area from which discussion questions and debate propositions emerge. Following that decision, the Committee's executive secretary edits a two-volume handbook on substantive aspects of the problem and, in addition, arranges for the preparation of bibliographies and the collection of authoritative materials that become available to individual schools through their state speech leagues on a reduced-cost or free-distribution basis. The Committee also carries on a number of other activities, including arranging for a national radio discussion involving authorities in the field and a debate between persons with equally broad experience and knowledge as part of the program of the joint national meeting of the Committee with the Speech Association of America. The resources of this Committee are available through membership in each of the state speech leagues or by direct contact with the executive secretary.

In the conduct of human affairs, discussion and debate often take place in formally organized meetings where the speaking is required to fit within the framework of procedural rules commonly accepted by the participants. Such a framework of rules is referred to, usually, as parliamentary procedure. Participants accept these rules either because they sincerely believe them to be the best set of rules applicable or because such rules have been established by the group in the past and their acceptance is required of anyone who wishes to join the group after it has been organized.

Parliamentary procedure is not limited, obviously, to specific types of meetings. What is less obvious, however, is the fact that parliamentary procedure is nothing more than an arbitrarily established set of rules. Different groups can function under different sets of such rules. There is no such thing as a universally accepted set of rules, although—because of the complexity of a system of this sort and the resultant difficulty of composing an original system— one set of rules may be much more widely used than others. This is, in fact, the case—which enables people to move from one group to another and participate, with some ease, in the deliberations of each group. In any group, however, the members should exercise care to be sure that they are familiar with the parliamentary procedural code within which the group functions.

The realization of parliamentary procedure as an arbitrary set of rules serves to underline the fact that it possesses no magic qualities; it in no way guarantees the success of the deliberations. In a sense, parliamentary procedure can be likened to a traffic control system. Both systems can labor under the burden of peak periods of activity. Both systems can break down because of the activities of those who are ignorant of the rules, willfully disobedient, or willing to follow only the letter and not the spirit of the law.

In a meeting in which there is much business to be conducted, the mechanics of parliamentary procedure may seem cumbersome at times. This is particularly true when the parliamentary procedure being followed includes what most people identify with such procedure—motions, seconds, amendments, discussion, and voting. Impressed with all the business to be conducted and the delays involved in conducting each individual item of business, some people are tempted to feel that, however democratic the process is, it is simply too inefficient. At such times, a variety of factors may contribute to the breaking down of the system. Actions may be taken not as a result of the best thinking of the group but merely because people are tired and want to go home. Or items of business may be taken care of outside the framework of the meeting with the meeting being used simply as a vehicle for informing the membership. Or items of business may receive no attention whatsoever, so that, in effect, the unconscious decision is made to take no action, to make no change, or to continue with an ongoing situation. Whenever the system breaks down for any of these specific reasons, there is an abandonment of the role of discussion and debate in problem solving—that is, there is an abandonment of the democratic process. Whether people are coerced into abandoning the democratic process or whether they voluntarily give it up because of apathy or because of reasons that seem to them at the moment to be justifiable, the abandonment is none the less real and should be recognized for what it is.

People who are ignorant of the rules cannot make the system function. They are incapable of protecting themselves from the activity of unprincipled people who are willing to take advantage of their ignorance. Those who are ignorant are also incapable of protecting themselves from their own confusion, with a resultant increase in the apparent inefficiency of parliamentary procedure. It is not at all uncommon, for example, to find groups of highly intelligent people becoming so snarled up in the machinery of parliamentary procedure—in a deliberation in which nobody is trying to take advantage of anybody—that during a close vote on an issue of importance many affirmative votes are cast by people who are actually opposed to the proposition for which they are voting. This is an excellent example of ignorance denying the advantages of the democratic process to an individual who is fully equipped except for his own failure to take advantage of opportunities available to him to overcome his ignorance.

There are, unfortunately, people who know the rules but who are sufficiently lacking in principle to be willing to break the rules. These people deliberately repudiate the democratic process for themselves and deny the advantages of it to others. Such people will make decisions apart from the group even in the knowledge that the procedural rules call for these decisions to be made by the group as a whole. Such people will seek to reach decisions on a majority vote even in the knowledge that the rules call for a two-thirds vote; or will demand a two-thirds majority before action is taken in the hope of confusing others into overlooking the fact that, for the matter in question, a simple majority is sufficient. The tactics of such people are not coped with merely by the presence of a knowledgeable parliamentarian whose advice can be sought when there is any question of the interpretation of the rules; what is also necessary is a membership that is knowledgeable about the rules, insistent that the rules be adhered to, and capable of articulating both their knowledge and their conviction.

Perhaps the greatest impediment to effective parliamentary procedure, however, is the inability of many people to recognize the need to accept the spirit as well as the letter of the rules involved in the system. What is necessary in any business meeting is a commitment on the part of the participants to the task of accomplishing the business which gives the members of the meeting a common organizational identity. With this commitment comes an acceptance of parliamentary procedure as a tool to facilitate the performance of the task at hand. The person who accepts parliamentary procedure as such a tool uses it only as he needs to use it. A man who recognizes a hammer as a tool does not insist on using it to pound upon everything in sight. Nor will he be averse, at times, to using it to straighten a nail rather than to drive it. Nor will he hesitate to replace the claw-hammer with a crowbar when the nail to be pulled is too long and too firmly held in place. The man who looks upon the hammer as a tool employs it in relation to the task; the same is true of the man who looks upon parliamentary procedure as a tool. In this regard, it may be pointed out that there are different-weight hammers among which meaningful choices may be made.

Similarly, the procedures of the Quaker business meeting—in which no formal motions are made and majority vote never determines the course of action—may be the most suitable procedure for the conduct of certain meetings; and a variety of other procedural systems may be best suited, individually and uniquely, to a variety of other meetings. But even within the most rigid and complex systems of parliamentary procedure, it is necessary that people do not digress even though there is no rule against digression; it is necessary that those contributing most actively to the amendments and the discussion shall not be permitted to amend and discuss without concern for the motion, other than a desire to postpone action on a motion scheduled to come up later for consideration.

In other words, parliamentary procedure should be employed to expedite the democratic process and not as a strategic weapon placed in the hands of those who would prevent the majority from reaching a decision or from taking an action. It is important to realize that such strategies can be engaged in by people who observe all the procedural rules and who are completely honest. Such people may follow the rules to the letter; they accept the machinery of democracy, but not its underlying philosophy. The proper functioning of parliamentary procedure, therefore, is dependent on the proper orientation of the people who employ it. If the orientation is incorrect, the system is doomed to fail, and no intellectual knowledge of the technicalities will save it. In this sense, it is quite possible to look upon the business meetings that are held throughout the United States in organizations that are social, religious, occupational, commercial, or governmental and gain some meaningful insight—from their method of conducting business—into the extent to which Americans are accepting the underlying philosophy of democracy or merely its machinery.

Broadcasting

Broadcasting is radio and television communication intended to be received by the public. Radio and television communication involves transmission and reception within a specific frequency range. The opportunity to employ such communication is limited. Unless transmitters operate within the framework of frequency-allocation controls, the signals they generate will interfere with each other and communication will be distorted or meaningless. Of the transmitters that can be placed in operation in any area, most serve non-broadcast purposes. Examples are ship-to-shore telephones, radio networks maintained by police and fire departments, industrial networks operated by railroads, power companies, taxicab and trucking services, and marine and aeronautical navigation systems. Frequencies available for broadcasting are necessarily limited. As a result, broadcasters do not operate in a freely competitive system. The desire and the financial resources are not, in themselves, sufficient to enable a broadcaster to transmit; he must also be allocated a permit to broadcast. In many instances, such a permit is not available on the purely technical grounds that all available frequencies are already in use. The ability to broadcast, then, is something of a privilege. Within the United States, the frequency spectrum within which broadcasters may transmit has been interpreted as being the property of the public; in return for the privilege of using such property for private profit, the broadcaster is considered to assume an ethical obligation to broadcast in the public interest. Administration of the technical and social controls of broadcasting has been placed, by law and organizational arrangement, in one of the several bureaus of the Federal Communications Commission. This bureau, through the Commission, is responsible to Congress and, ultimately, to the people.

The American educational system has three major interests in broadcasting. The simplest to understand, although possibly the least important, is training in radio and television production. In addition, and of much more vital importance, is training in radio and television consumption. Finally, the educational system has to concern itself with its own utilization, actual or potential, of radio and television.

Many people are employed, professionally, in broadcasting. In training people for gainful employment, education can include within its scope the training of broadcasting personnel. The personnel needs of broadcasting are varied and demand many different training backgrounds. In addition to differences in area of specialization, there are also differences in the amount and level of training required of the various personnel. Speech and theater educators can address themselves, meaningfully, to only some of the needs at different levels of education. Within the framework of a social philosophy that considers the democratic function to depend on an informed citizenry, it is desirable that every qualified citizen achieve a college education. In this sense, the television cameraman—as an American citizen—would profit from a college education; as a television cameraman, however, his "specialized" training could be achieved, quite satisfactorily, in an intensive technical school program. What contribution can speech and theater make to the "specialized" training of broadcasting personnel? A knowledge of the techniques, purposes, and responsibilities of speech communication is one contribution. Another contribution is a mastery of theater as an art form. Who is best equipped to help the student adapt his speech and theater training to the broadcast medium? This question has been answered, by educators, in several ways. One answer calls for a professional broadcaster with a formal or practical background in speech and theater. Another answer calls for a speech and theater educator with a background in broadcasting. A third answer calls for a supervisor of a production-laboratory facility in which the student learns how to make the adaptation through his own trial and error. The third answer seems to be most consistent with modern theories of learning.

All Americans are related to broadcasting, directly or indirectly, as consumers. Even the individual who avoids both radio and television lives in a society in which the tastes, values, concepts, and habits of those about him are influenced by broadcasting. For this reason, everyone has a vested interest in broadcasting. To protect that interest, the individual must understand what broadcasting is, how it functions, the legal, social, and economic framework within which it operates, his own relationship to it, and the channels available to him for exerting some influence on the way it operates. In this regard, it would be well for educated members of American society to develop standards and techniques for the evaluation of the content as well as the techniques of broadcasting and to have the perspective that comes from the ability to examine broadcasting within the framework of a larger understanding of world broadcasting and of mass-media communication.

As a medium of rapid communication to large numbers of people, broadcasting has a recognized educational potential. Educational systems in the United States and in many other parts of the world have reacted by taking advantage of this potential in numerous ways. There is considerable literature and research on the subject of instructional television, despite the fact that much of the activity in this area is still exploratory in nature. Even less attention is being paid to the even greater and perhaps more significant potential of broadcasting to contribute to the task of continuing education, however. In a world going through a profound and rapid technological and scientific revolution, it is vitally necessary that education be considered an ongoing process with no formal terminal point. This is not only true for the physician employing drugs that were unknown to medical science during the period of his medical training; it is equally true for the citizen expected to influence political decision-making regarding nations, people, and problems far different from what he learned about during his formal education. American education, in general, has failed to come to grips with this problem. The American educational system struggles under the burden of providing formal education without adequate resources, to say nothing of undertaking the additional burden of providing the machinery for continuing education. More basic than this, however, is the failure of American education to inculcate in the students whom it trains any real understanding of the need for such continuing education or any motivation to achieve it. In a world in flux, too many college graduates in America consider their education complete with the granting of whatever degree is associated with the field in which they desire to work. It is not surprising, therefore, that too little attention is paid to broadcasting's potential in continuing education.

Interpretation

Interpretation is the reading aloud of literature so as to share with the audience the reader's response to and appreciation of the literary work. Interpretation involves, therefore, a high degree of responsiveness to the literary work and the ability to employ speech effectively in stimulating a comparable responsiveness in the audience. The interpreter most commonly reads from manuscript, but he may read from memory. Unlike the actor, the interpreter does not lose his own identity in that of some literary character. The interpreter provides speech stimuli that enable the members of the audience to create mental images. When the people, places, and actions of a literary work come to life during an interpretative reading, they come to life in the individual imaginations of the audience members.

One of the educational values of interpretation is derived from the literary material. The student's detailed study of the literature is motivated by his necessity to be fully responsive to what he would share with others. He sees the literature in its communicative dimension just because he approaches it with the intent of employing it communicatively. He is forced to examine every detail because he must present every detail when he reads it aloud. Perhaps most important because of its uniqueness, however, he must follow through from analysis to synthesis. Most formal literary study emphasizes literary analysis and leaves to the student a synthesis that is necessary to complete appreciation but that is, unfortunately, often neglected. Interpretation demands synthesis, however. The interpreter must react to the totality of the literature while he is engaged in the process of stimulating an audience to respond to that totality.

Another educational value of interpretation is derived from its employment of speech. Interpretation motivates the development of speech expressiveness. Interpretative analysis is distinct from literary analysis just to the extent that the former focuses attention on how speech is to be used in sharing the insights achieved, in large measure, through the latter. The interpreter, then, develops expressive speech and employs it in communicating to an audience.

To realize the educational values of interpretation, care must be exercised to avoid a number of potential dangers. The concept of the nature of interpretation must not be distorted. The study of the literature must not fail to consider all the persons involved in the communicative act. The speech techniques must not be considered other than as means to an end, and the end must not be misconceived.

The nature of interpretation is frequently misunderstood. When it is not limited to literature, the materials used are often of no intrinsic value and lead to a waste of student time. When it is confused with acting, an artificial limitation is imposed on the nature of the literature that can be utilized.

Those involved in the communicative act of interpretation are the author, the interpreter, and the members of the audience. The interpreter has an ethical responsibility to the author that is fulfilled only by an honest and thorough attempt to be fully responsive to the author's work. The teacher who assists a student of interpretation should not insist that there is only one correct way to understand a literary selection. The teacher should insist, however, that the student's understanding be the result of conscientious and thorough investigation, that it reflect knowledge and sensitivity, that it possess consistency, and that the student be at ease in defending it.

The interpreter will not be able to achieve a fully responsible relationship to the author of every literary work. The interpreter, therefore, must have some freedom of choice. This does not imply that the student interpreter should select only works that are simple to understand. On the contrary, the student will learn most from what demands the most—provided that the demand is reasonable rather than excessive. The interpreter, then, should work with literature that is within the range of his sensitivity and comprehension, although comprehension may come only as the result of prolonged and difficult study. How prolonged and difficult the study can be will depend on the interpreter's motivation.

Interpretative communication exists only when an audience responds. The nature of audience response is dependent not only on the selection of the literary material and the comprehension and skill of the interpreter, but on the sensitivity and understanding of the audience itself. This means that the interpreter, like the public speaker, must engage in audience analysis and must keep the audience in mind in the selection and preparation of an interpretative reading as well as in the reading itself.

With regard to speech techniques, it is vital that the interpreter realize that speech is a means to the end of a shared response to the literature. The focus of audience attention should be on the literature, not on the interpreter as a person or as a technician. In interpretation, as in any art, the techniques should be concealed. As with any art, interpretation requires techniques that are artificial and that, in the early stages of preparation, may be handled quite mechanically. Some who confuse insincerity with artifice shun technique; but this is comparable to refusing the pianist the use of a metronome or the painter the conscious study of perspective. The point is that techniques should be mastered to the point of requiring no conscious attention by either interpreter or audience during the communicative act.

Theater

Educational theater is theatrical production within an educational institution which is designed to contribute to the educational objectives of that institution. It may well be that admission fees are charged and that income is necessary to support or expand the theatrical activity. Those who devote their time and energies to production may aim at a high level of artistic achievement. Nonetheless, educational theater justifies its existence on the basis of the educational contribution which it makes.

What are the educational contributions? One is the training of theater artists. Another is the bringing to life of dramatic literature. Another is the provision of an activity that offers benefits in speech training, recreation, and personality development.

Educational theater provides an excellent training facility for aspiring theater artists. In educational theater, students can learn each of the arts associated with theater production not only individually but in relation to one another and to the totality of production. This is true in unequal degrees for various arts, however. The opportunity to do acting or almost all types of technical theater work is usually much greater than the opportunity to design, direct, or write. There is also opportunity, although somewhat more limited than for acting or technical production work, to integrate the art of music or dance into theatrical production; here, too, the opportunity is greater for developing interpretative talents than for promoting the creative talents of composition and choreography.

Educational theater is the only legitimate theater in many communities and in many regions throughout the United States. It provides the opportunity for audiences to see dramatic literature as it was intended to be seen. Educational theater provides a wide range of dramatic literature. In fact, from the standpoint of maintaining a cultural heritage, the educational theater probably contributes more than any other type of theater in the United States.

Acting makes great demands on speech expressiveness. Working to achieve the necessary clarity of enunciation, projection, meaningfulness, and emotional expressiveness is excellent training in speech. Actors also frequently benefit from the psychological impact of bringing a character to life on the stage and sensing the responsiveness of the audience to that character. The experience of holding an audience "spellbound" for a moment is an exhilarating one. In addition to the personal satisfaction which this provides, the actor often emerges with an increased poise and sense of self-confidence. In the process of preparation, of course, the actors and all others working on the production develop a sense of cooperativeness, learn the importance of assuming responsibilities, and generally enjoy the sociability of group activity.

The achievement of all these objectives within the educational theater is not simple. The training values are achieved only if the director and the technical director know their business, know how to teach, and are willing to teach. The director who views actors as robots or as polished performers is not apt to teach very much. The technical director who is a perfectionist and prefers to build things himself for the sake of having them better built is not apt to teach very much. Achieving the training values makes other demands on the educators involved. There must be a good mixture of plays, providing a variety of production problems. Opportunity must be given to students with varying degrees of talent and experience. In this regard, note may be made of the fact that educational theater is doing little to nurture developing playwrights.

In fulfilling its role of bringing dramatic literature to life, educational theater should take advantage of the entire range of that literature, carefully avoiding provincialism. Drama produced should represent all parts of the world, all periods of time, all theatrical styles, all points of view, and all modes of expression.

As a speech-training activity, educational theater should maintain the highest standards possible with regard to vocal expressiveness; and directors should be able not only to call for the best, but to teach students how to achieve it. To maximize the personality and recreational values, educational theater should bring students into contact with educators of sensitivity and integrity. Within the framework of its basic objectives, there is scant room in the educational theater for temperamental directors with little respect for human values or human dignity.

The flourishing educational theater is extremely broad in scope, providing both the production personnel and the audiences with a variety of experiences. As opportunity presents itself, productions should be staged in proscenium theaters, in outdoor theaters, and in the round—that is, with the audience seated on all sides of the acting area. Plays should include tragedy, serious drama, melodrama, farce, comedy, satire, musicals, and opera. Children's theater should present plays to audiences of children. The plays should be written for children and acted by adults, by children, and by both together. Opportunity should exist for creative dramatics in which child actors evolve the characterizations and the actions of the play by themselves as they rehearse. Experimental theater should provide facilities needed to try out new scripts and unusual acting, designing, and directing techniques, to produce plays of historical interest but of extremely limited appeal, and to offer experience in all aspects of production to people of creativity and imagination who are in the process of developing their talents.

CHAPTER VII

Speech Education: Evaluation and Improvement

Standards

To evaluate speech, to determine where improvement is called for and the relative seriousness of various deficiencies, it is necessary to establish certain norms or standards. In seeking such norms, different levels of acceptability should be recognized. One level may be described as that of speech communication fundamentals, another as informal speech communication, a third as public speech communication.

Speech communication fundamentals are minimal requirements without which speech cannot succeed in accomplishing its basic communicative function. The minimal requirements are audibility, clarity, significance, and vitality. Audibility is a matter of volume level or projection. Audibility is sufficient when every member of the audience can hear everything that the speaker says. Keeping in mind the visible speech code, this might be enlarged to include a minimal requirement that, when the speaker uses visual reinforcement, every member of the audience can see whatever the speaker does. Clarity is a matter of going beyond hearing or seeing to an understanding of what is heard or seen. Without clarity, there is no understanding and no stimulation of meaning.

Significance is distinguished from clarity in that the latter relates to the response to speech elements while the former relates to the response to connected speech. Clarity is a matter of precise articulation of individual words. Significance is a matter of interrelationships of grouped words employing the code system of a particular language for expressive purposes. Significance is commonly taken to include value judgments regarding the expressive purposes. To the extent that speech is considered a part of formal education, it seems appropriate to demand more of the speaker, even minimally, than mere audibility and clarity. Educators should include, in addition, significance—in the sense of expressive purpose as well as of interrelated language elements. Again, in the interests of not setting minimal standards too low, speech education should insist on vitality. That is, a speaker should reflect, in his expression, a personal involvement in what he is saying and an energetic drive to communicate with his audience.

How the speaker should conduct himself is influenced by the interrelationship between himself and the speaking situation. An informal speaking situation is quite distinct from more formal situations. This is reflected in the content and style of the speaker. The more informal the situation, the easier it is for the speaker to assess the reactions of his audience. Informality makes for intimacy and a greater freedom of expression—not only for the speaker but for the audience in indicating its response. Since the whole purpose of speech communication is to stir up responses, the speaker profits greatly from audience feedback that indicates the nature of what he is succeeding in stirring up. The speaker should seek, therefore, to encourage informality—whenever this is appropriate—by his choice of words, sentence structures, use of images or analogies, physical behavior, or any other stylistic elements that are helpful. Conversational speech is generally impromptu—spontaneous. In informal speaker-audience situations, the speaker should strive for extemporaneous delivery, following a pre-planned sequence of ideas but expressing these ideas in words that occur to him in the communicative situation itself. Extemporaneous delivery allows the speaker to be much more responsive to his audience. The extemporaneous speaker, if sufficiently skilled, should even be free to deviate from his pre-planned sequence of ideas. In this way, not only style but the very content of the speech may grow out of the communicative situation.

In more formal speaking situations, there is usually less interplay between the speaker and the audience. There is, as a result, less opportunity to assess audience response and to adapt to that response. The more formal the situation is, the less opportunity there is for adaptation in the process of speaking, and the greater is the temptation to pre-plan a great deal of the speech. Such preplanning may include the composition of the entire speech in advance and the delivery of the speech from a manuscript. Formality, of course, does not impair the type of adaptation to an audience that is done in advance of the actual communication, such as choice of topic, selection of illustrations, and decisions as to the appropriateness of humor. To the contrary, speech composition must occur with the audience in mind and, as the ability to make adjustments during delivery decreases, the preliminary adaptation becomes more important. The preliminary adaptation, of course, will be affected by the formality of the occasion, as evidenced by the formality of style and of presentation.

In addition to the standards that relate to levels of acceptability, there are also standards of vocal usage that relate to the geographic and cultural area within which speech communication occurs. In the United States, cultured and educated speakers are assumed to employ one of three speech standards—General American, Eastern, or Southern. The Southern standard is the method of speaking— primarily a matter of articulation, pronunciation, and inflection— associated with the cultured, educated people of those states roughly approximating the old Confederacy. The Eastern standard is the speech pattern associated with the cultured, educated people of the New England and middle Atlantic seaboard states. The General American standard is the speech pattern associated with the cultured, educated people of the remainder of the country. No one of these three standards is inherently superior or inferior to the others. The choice of the standard is, theoretically, a matter of the area of the country with which the speaker wishes to be identified. In actual practice, the proper standard for a given individual is usually determined by the geographic circumstances of his birth, rearing, and place of habitation. Although a person can consciously change from one speech standard to another, it is difficult for an adult to replace habits of speech formed as a child and established by years of repetition.

Many people speak with substandard patterns that are the result of regional or local deviations. Such deviations give the general impression that the speaker is not cultured and educated. Clearly, culture and education do not always result in standard speech; nor is standard speech a sure sign of culture and education. Speech patterns are superficial elements capable of being changed. The difficulty of changing such patterns, however, suggests that they are much less superficial than is, for example, clothing. With respect to such elements as clothing, cleaniness, and neatness, the average person recognizes the importance of the impression made by superficials. This is reflected in the pains taken with dress and grooming in preparing for a date, a job interview, or an initial contact with a certain group of people. With respect to the less superficial element of speech, at least equal pains should be taken. The failure to attend to speech as to grooming is, in large part, the result of insensitivity to the degree to which speech contributes to the general impression that a person makes on others. The failure is, perhaps more fundamentally, the result of ignorance as to the possibility of making changes and the procedures for doing so.

On what basis should a speaker determine the proper standard or choose to be content with a particular substandard variation? The answer is, perhaps, not so much one of geography as of culture. The speaker should employ the speech patterns of his community. This is a meaninful concept if "community" is taken to be a definition of the people with whom the speaker identifies himself rather than of the area within which the speaker lives. In this sense, several people living in the same geographic area can live in different communities. When a speaker's standard or substandard speech is the same as that of his audience, the audience members identify the speaker as one of the group. Some speakers, indeed, have developed the relatively rare facility of shifting back and forth—often subconsciously—between several speech patterns, depending on the group with whom they are speaking and identifying themselves. When the speaker's standard or substandard speech is different from that of the audience, the amount of difference will make the speech patterns more or less distracting. A slight distraction may add charm or even lend authority—as when an analysis of a foreign country is presented by a speaker whose accent reveals him to be a native of the country about which he speaks. A great deal of distraction may result in the audience paying less attention to what is said than to how it is said. Much distraction may even extend to the point of real difficulty of comprehension. The question for the individual speaker is to determine the groups in which he wishes to speak with complete identification and the groups in which he wishes to communicate effectively without undue distraction. In this regard, it may be well to point out that any one of the three standards is clearly comprehensible and free of distraction for speakers of either of the other standards. It is also true that standard speech may be a distraction to speakers of certain substandard variants.

Standards of speech are important in their effect on the purposes and applications of speech communication. These can be described as including the achievement of adjustive, vocational, societal, and artistic objectives.

Adjustive speech communication conditions the individual's personal integration with his environment. A person evaluates others on the basis of their speech. A person is evaluated by others on the basis of his own speech. This goes beyond the establishment of community identification already discussed; it includes personality concepts. As for community identification, a word may be added to the earlier mention of the fact that it is possible not only to change identification but to shift back and forth between identifications. This is not uncommon in an individual who was born and reared in one environment and who then completely changed his evironment. An example of this would be the politician who campaigns in the backwoods using a speech pattern that identifies him as having been born and raised there but who, among his colleagues in the state capitol, speaks with little or no trace of his backwoods origin. In spite of the obvious advantages of such an arrangement, it is usually not the result of any conscious planning but simply a matter of falling back into old habits or reassuming the more newly acquired habits in response to the prevailing practices of those in the immediate environment.

As for personality concepts, there is value in considering, therefore, the nature of the insights provided or the impressions made by speech. Examples of this would be the pleasant voice as contrasted to the gruff voice, the complaining characteristics of certain types of nasality, the way in which use of rate and force suggests degrees of energy and animation, and the difference between clear, forceful, poised delivery on the one hand and hesitant, mumbled delivery on the other.

Vocational speech communication facilitates coordinated activity on the job. Much of the official communication establishing procedures, indicating the work to be accomplished, or actually enabling the work to be done occurs through speech. It is highly desirable that such speech meet minimal requirements of being both precise and concise. Precision makes for effective communication.

Conciseness enables communication to occur without undue curtailment of the time needed to perform the activity that the communication seeks to facilitate. In addition, since communication is among people, it is desirable that the speech standards be such as to facilitate pleasant interrelationships. A concise and precise speech communication may be weakened in its effectiveness by the irritating emotional response that is stimulated by the form rather than the content of the communication.

Societal speech communication meets the need that may exist for enabling certain societal institutions to function. Such institutions may be the exceedingly informal social organizations of bridge clubs, occupationally related organizations such as labor unions, chambers of commerce, and professional associations, or the legally created and precisely structured organizations of government on all levels. Societal speech communication exists in the activities of inter-governmental relationships as well.

Minimal standards for such speech communication are somewhat complex. Beyond audibility, clarity, significance, and vitality, beyond appropriateness of content, style, and identification, beyond personal adjustment, precision, and conciseness, there is a threefold need to understand the purpose of the institution, to understand the framework of operational procedures within which the institutional business is conducted (including, for example, its accepted code of parliamentary procedure), and to apply the principle of audience adaptation. However desirable or even necessary audience adaptation may be in other speech situations, it should be viewed as a minimum requirement for societal speech. In this application, stress should be placed not so much on the techniques by which adaptation is effected as on the ability to comprehend the responses of others in terms of their point of view, their background, their values, and their sensitivities. Without this comprehension, there is insufficient motivation for the seeking out and the application of the adaptation techniques. With this comprehension, not only will adaptation occur but it will take precedence over the other speech elements. In other words, there will be times when speech communication will be more effective just because it is less precise, less concise, sometimes even less significant in its content if not in its impact.

When speech communication moves into this area of subtle refinements where principles or rules seem to be set aside and communication is "played by ear," it may appear that speech has become more of an art than anything else. In point of fact, speech can function as an art and, to achieve its fullest impact and make its greatest contribution to human interaction, must function as an art. This is as true for the conversationalist or the persuasive speaker as it is for the interpretative reader or the actor. The standards of artistic speech are necessarily complex and subject to considerable conflict of opinion because of the role played by subjective judgment. Standards of artistic speech, therefore, are best considered in terms of evaluative, critical, and interpretative estimates rather than in terms of minimal requirements.

Adaptation to Social and Individual Needs

Speech standards must be viewed not only as theoretical abstractions, but as related both to the changing needs of society and to the varying levels of individual proficiency and potential. Increasing social and vocational complexity, mass communication, and population mobility have had their effects on what educators define as the normal, superior, and handicapped student in speech. Those abilities and skills which served past generations well may be inadequate for the individual in today's world. Science and technology have extended and intensified the impact of man's oldest tool, human speech. No longer are we confined to reading and direct conversation as sources of information exchange and intellectual stimulation. The telephone, radio, talking pictures, and television have made the African tribesman and the Washington diplomat common participants in the affairs of the world. Current political developments, scientific accomplishments, symphony orchestras, Shakespearian drama, and instantaneous reports from remote geographical areas are available at the turn of a dial. As these media transmit human speech, they change our teaching methods, news distribution, salesmanship, religious persuasion, political campaigning, and patterns of family life.

Superior skill in speech has always been essential for intellectual and political leaders. Only as the frontier disappeared, the population increased, and our democratic society became more complex did the mass of people have extensive need for such ability. One hundred years ago, informal conversation and some ability in economic bargaining served the average man well. Skill with animals and simple tools, coupled with adaptation to new and sometimes harsh conditions of frontier life, were necessary for his survival. Ability with the gun, the axe, and the plow were the measures of his success. He listened to his leaders and responded with his vote and his movement to the West.

Today we find little if any use for the hallmarks of the earlier period. Our success depends increasingly on communicating effectively about ideas, persons, goods, services, relationships, laws, education, and international understanding. All these require ability in speech.

As the individual's oral communication has increased in quantity and complexity, limitations or deviations which seemed bothersome in the simple society of his grandfather now prove to be major handicaps. In fact, the very dynamics of contemporary society may accentuate these and be the source of additional difficulties. Thus, the concept of what constitutes appropriate speech instruction for a wide range of students is a unique problem that does not lend itself to the same analysis as may be applied to many other subject areas. For example, the mathematics that is essential for the individual's social and vocational survival may perhaps be mastered by the sixth grade, with trigonometry and elementary calculus being reserved for the unusual student who will eventually emerge as a scientist or engineer. The parallel does not necessarily apply to the individual's communicative behavior; those who perform the most menial of tasks must continue to have a social existence, to live cooperatively with the very able in a democratic society, and to carry on some type of meaningful communication as part of their economic activities.

If there is a place in the education of all American youth for the study of speech, how is this instruction to be planned so that the student may meet the appropriate standards of communication and adapt the training to his individual needs? In answering such a question, we must recognize that changes are taking place, not only in the composition of the student body in the schools but in the demands and standards for communicative effectiveness which they must meet. Legislation, social pressures, and economic necessity have combined to make high school attendance and graduation the common educational pattern. Beyond that, an increasing number of graduates are considering college. Some estimates suggest that within the decade one out of every two high school graduates will attempt some type of college program. The wide variations in student abilities, motivations, and goals have been reflected in the secondary-school curricula. These variations also present challenging problems to those responsible for the courses and activities in speech. What program of instruction should be provided for all, and what special provision should be made for both the superior and the handicapped student? The answer depends in part on our concept of what constitutes superior and handicapped students. The lines of demarcation are not sharply defined, and the standards or groupings may vary among schools or areas.

It is possible to make functional classifications if we consider the superior or gifted student as one having some of the following qualities or characteristics: high intellectual ability, deep interest in the subject, strong motivations, demonstrated excellence in communication, and potential for continued growth and development. In contrast, two approaches may be used in defining the speech-handicapped student. To the extent that a student falls below accepted norms for his age and maturity, he may be considered handicapped, and the diagnosis may change with time and circumstance. A functional approach evaluates the student's communicative effectiveness. Thus, he may fail to meet some of the standards discussed in the first section of this chapter and still compensate in other ways so as to remain a relatively adequate communicator. He could be considered handicapped, however, to the extent that it was not possible for him to approach his potential effectiveness after his obvious handicaps were removed or corrected.

Whatever basis of definition is used, it should be noted that low intelligence is not necessarily a characteristic of the speech-handicapped child. In certain cases, intelligence will be a factor, but the factors affecting speech are so diverse that the child of high intelligence may experience difficulties equal to, or greater than, those of his less gifted peers. For purposes of this discussion, we may say that a student is handicapped in oral communication when his speech reflects those qualities and characteristics that adversely affect his communication with others or when his hearing is so impaired as to affect his reception of oral messages or as to affect his own production of speech. Such handicaps may range from minor acoustic variations (for example, lisping) to deep-seated psychological disorders (for example, stuttering) or organic difficulties (for example, cleft palate). Whatever may be the unique factors that set any group of individuals apart, all members of the group have the common need to develop their maximum communicative potential as a means of personal, social, and economic adjustment.

Speech Education for the Normal Student

The normal student can profit from a curricular and co-curricular program as presented in Chapter III. At this point it is merely necessary to emphasize that, for such a student, the major orientation is functional and cultural.

The functional orientation leads to a focus on the application of speech skills to day-to-day living. In this respect, the teacher must avoid too strong a focus on the "artistic" side of speech. Such a focus may lead many students into the dangerously erroneous concept that speech is an exotic subject for people with unique talents. In this respect, too, the teacher must evaluate and work for improvement within the framework of the abilities and sensitivities of those who do not possess unique talents. While the teacher of speech is understandably attracted, as is any teacher, to the gifted student, there must be a clear and continuous dedication to the needs of those constituting the great majority whose gifts are not unique, but human.

The cultural orientation leads to a focus on the speech arts from the standpoint of consumption and recreation rather than from that of professional performance. Clearly, the standards of evaluation and the emphasis placed on procedures for improvement will not be the same for the embryonic actor as for the embryonic businessman, who, hopefully, will enjoy good theater and who may find the time and motivation to participate in a community or church theater group.

Speech Education for the Superior Student

In addition to basic training, enriched courses and special programs should be provided for students with special abilities and potentials. Social efficiency dictates that the capacities be developed and utilized appropriately. It is from those of superior ability that a high percentage of our potential leaders in all areas will emerge. It is important that such persons be maximally effective in their oral communication. These students generally possess great capacity for self-expression, personal development, and creativity. Some find their life work in fields where their special speech talents are particularly useful, such as law, social work, government, broadcasting, theater, teaching, and lecturing. Others find use for their abilities as leaders of their colleagues and official spokesmen and interpreters in such diverse areas of work as science, business management, and legislation. Still others find avocational and service outlets in their communities and social organizations.

Superior students must, of necessity, understand and master the same basic curricular program as must the normal individuals. They should, however, have opportunities to deepen their understanding and to refine, polish, and perfect their skills. It is to be expected that they may progress more rapidly, perhaps omitting some steps or stages. Not only should they have opportunity to enroll in elective courses, but there should be enriched or advanced sections available to them. Superior students should not only have opportunity for special projects within their classes; they should try their hand at planning, directing, and presenting intra-school programs. They will also normally be interested in inter-school activities such as competitions, Speakers' Bureau work, and public programs. They have the capacity not only to work with their peers in speech, but to engage in cooperative activities with other students in other subject areas, as well as with faculty and adults beyond the school. In short, they should have opportunity to experience a wide variety of interesting and challenging communicative experiences.

While superior students normally will be attracted to inter-school activities and to positions of leadership, they should not monopolize these roles. Many normal and even some handicapped students may profit greatly from such work. The school is an appropriate place for those of different communicative abilities and potentials to gain experience in working together in a democratic manner in all spheres of communicative activity that have social and personal value, both during school and in later life.

Within recent years an increasing number of summer high school speech institutes have developed, most of which are designed specifically for the superior student whose interests are in forensics, dramatics, or broadcasting. Sponsored by colleges and universities, these provide from three to five weeks of intensive, specialized study under the direction of highly qualified and experienced teachers from both the secondary and the collegiate levels. Admission policies vary, some institutes being limited to residents of a given state and others having open enrollment. The smallest may enroll twenty students; the larger, over one hundred. Some place a limit on the number admitted and attract many more than are enrolled. The great majority of institute programs are academically challenging; the student who possesses the ability, motivation, and maturity to respond will gain much from living and working with a group of equally outstanding young men and women.

One of the most recent innovations has been the resident assembly program, as initiated by the University of Minnesota and more recently encouraged by the American Assembly. Here, again, specially selected students from schools throughout a state or area are brought together for two or three days to study, discuss, and formulate recommendations concerning a particular public issue. Such projects require careful planning, appropriate facilities, and adequate financial support. The benefits to the students involved and to their schools—plus the potential social values—fully justify such efforts.

Rehabilitation of the
Speech-Handicapped Student

We may be certain that speech difficulties have existed since man began speaking. Early Egyptian records report "cures" for persons suffering speech impairments. Intentionally or otherwise, every teacher and every school does something about the speech difficulties of the five to ten per cent of students so handicapped. The questions are, what constitutes a speech difficulty, what can and should the teacher and the school do about it, and what procedures should be employed?

We have already presented a general concept of the speech-handicapped student. More specifically, the student is considered to be handicapped when: (1) his speech is so deviant as to make a difference that causes the listener to pay more attention to how the child speaks than to what he says; (2) the speech is difficult or impossible to understand; or (3) the speaker himself reacts to his utterance in such a way as to affect his communication adversely.

Avoiding the technical terminology of the pathologist and audiologist in favor of practical categories that have meaning to the speech correctionist, classroom teacher, and administrator, the abnormal speech encountered in the classroom is generally classified as follows:

1. Defects of articulation;
2. Defects of voice;
3. Stuttering;
4. Retarded speech development;
5. Speech difficulties related to physical (including brain) damage;
6. Speech problems related to auditory impairments.

There is no general agreement as to whether a seventh category, difficulties associated with symbolization or language as found among young children, should be recognized. It is also possible to classify difficulties as to primary source, some being functional and others organic. In some circumstances it may be difficult, if not impossible, to affect neat separations or divisions. For example, it is quite possible for an organic condition that is only indirectly related to an individual's speech to be a contributing source to a psychological condition, which, in turn, is related to a functional speech disorder.

Within any category or system of classification, a wide variety of manifestations and severity of problems may be found. Depending on the social standards, the minor difficulties associated with articulation, voice, impaired hearing, or retarded development in early childhood may be considered unimportant in one group while they occasion much concern in another. For example, the articulatory deviations of sound omissions (*pay* for *play*), sound substitutions (*twuck* for *truck*), or sound distortions may be the center of attention in one environment and go unnoticed in another. Articulatory difficulties may arise from organic conditions, faulty training, or faulty learning. They are also functions of age and maturation. Some estimates for children in the lower grades place the incidence of articulatory difficulties at from ten to twenty-five per cent. It is generally agreed that five per cent of the school population experience difficulties that merit special attention, and that from two to three per cent have problems of a serious nature.

Chronic voice difficulties are found relatively infrequently among children, although they are more common than is generally recognized. Principal problems of this sort relate to vocal changes at puberty, irritations associated with common colds or laryngitis, and difficulties associated with enlarged adenoids. At a later age, the individual with a harsh or husky voice may encounter little communication difficulty in one area of work yet find this quality a severe handicap in another.

Approximately from six to ten of every thousand school children show evidences of stuttering, boys having a slightly higher incidence than girls. It is seldom that the stutterer can conceal his difficulty; there are few circumstances in which its effect is not felt by both the speaker and the listener. Some authorities consider stuttering one of the most challenging of all speech problems.

The determination of what constitutes retarded speech development may be difficult when the child is very young. It is sometimes associated with mental subnormality, severe illness or physical defects, inadequate or inappropriate speech or communication environment, or particular traumatic experiences associated with communication.

Organic conditions such as cleft palate and brain injury (for example, cerebral palsy) often adversely affect physical and personality factors beyond communication. Minor impairments may appear unimportant unless the individual is placed in particular situations. Major, uncorrected difficulties will obviously affect the social and economic life of the individual.

Children with some significant hearing problem constitute an important group within our schools. Preliminary studies suggest that as many as nine per cent have medical problems that presently or potentially may affect hearing. The hearing levels of about five per cent of American school-age children are not normal; about twenty per cent of this group require special educational attention. Included in this last figure are approximately 25,000 classified as deaf.

A variety of discovery and diagnostic procedures are available. Where the difficulties are clearly revealed in the appearance or behavior of the child—or where he has been under medical or similar observation—examination, diagnosis, and rehabilitative procedures may be instituted prior to school enrollment. If highly specialized individual care and treatment are indicated, the case may never reach the general public or parochial schools. In some instances, however, special provisions through teachers and classes are made for children with unique or severe handicaps. When a speech and hearing rehabilitation program is to be initiated, standard practice is to survey the entire school population to locate, categorize, and determine a priority of need for those students having difficulties. Once this has been done, an annual check on new students coming into the system will keep the program up to date. Implied in the above arrangement is the establishment of appropriate criteria for making judgments as to both the existence of a difficulty and the procedures to be applied in dealing with it.

Evaluation of the Speech Program

The speech program itself should be evaluated and improved. The primary focus of all instruction in speech is the individual, and our concern is with the creation of those conditions for both learning and its application that will contribute to maximum personal development and effectiveness. It is clearly established that maximum improvement takes place in a soundly conceived and effectively executed instructional program. We must ask, then, what kinds of programs exist in our schools, and how effectively are they meeting the needs and potentials outlined earlier in this chapter?

It is true that an increasing number of schools are including some type of speech instruction; but, as a whole, the American educational system has failed to provide adequately for such needs or to recognize fully the potentials of programs of speech instruction. Too frequently, observation that an individual communicates in such a way as to effect some social adjustment is accepted as evidence of adequacy and justification for omission or termination of training.

Speech training is particularly important in the elementary-school curriculum; yet such instruction in general is provided only on an incidental or minimal basis. Increasing attention is being given to the discovery and correction of speech handicaps at that level, but no comparable concern is shown for communication training for either the average or the gifted students.

Many schools allege that they meet student needs through some type of co-curricular activity. Elective courses, particularly at the senior high school level, are becoming increasingly numerous. These do not, however, reach the majority of students; viewed in the broadest perspective, they do not provide adequate opportunity or training for the average students, particularly for those who have the greatest need for or who might profit most from such training.

Recognizing the importance of speech in their daily lives and having been denied appropriate training, many adults have sought it, at times, from superficial and often unethical programs taught by inadequately prepared individuals. The values of many such programs are questionable; they have helped spread abroad the false notion that speech can be taught with little effort in a few easy lessons.

Although administrators frequently contend that the development of adequate speech programs is limited by the number of available well-trained teachers, the gap between supply and demand is being closed. Concurrently, the major professional associations in the field have recognized that sound program development is in part dependent upon some national consensus as to principles and guidelines. Philosophical, empirical, and experimental justification must be found with respect to the concepts to be taught, the levels at which these are to be introduced, the methods and activities to be employed, and the standards of knowledge and proficiency to be expected. Such a basic continuing study has been given first priority by the Speech Association of America through its Committee on Curricula and Certification. The objective of instruction in speech must be adequate opportunity and facilities to make possible the maximum appropriate communicative development of each child under the direction of appropriately trained subject-matter specialists. The goal is still distant, but it is worthy of the consideration and coordinated efforts of administrators, curriculum planners, and subject-matter specialists.

A Look Forward in Speech Education

While human communication remains as significant, complex, pervasive, and diverse as ever, it also continues to both affect and be affected by changing social relationships. Although the purposes remain essentially unchanged, the ways of studying, teaching, viewing, and applying speech and its related areas are presently in flux.

Prophecy is accompanied by certain inherent dangers and carries with it some presumption; yet a few trends are discernible and merit attention. Within the next decade some, if not all, of the following developments may be expanded or intensified:

1. All segments of the public may be expected to become increasingly aware of the importance of speech. In an ever more complex society, where both individuals and groups must communicate frequently on matters of vital importance, the role of this medium must be understood and valued. The potential of the individual leader and the possibilities of mass instruction and persuasion bring home to all but the most insensitive the role which speech—including listening—plays in the life of the individual and the preservation of the culture.

2. The role or application of speech in our contemporary society will continue to undergo changes. As the numbers of individuals increase, as their multiple-group memberships expand, and as their welfare and security become dependent on increasingly diverse factors, the possibility of their direct communication with those individuals or groups that might affect their destinies is decreased. Thus, more people may find it necessary to communicate—particularly about economic and political matters—as members of a group rather than as individuals. As widely divergent cultures interact, sometimes threatening the security of the more advanced groups, an increasing burden of explanation, education, and persuasion must be borne by the spoken word. Such communication may range from the person-to-person conversation of the Peace Corps representative through planned instructional programs to massive persuasive barrages broadcast on a round-the-clock basis. In contrast, and at a different level, it may be that with increased leisure time, speech will become in larger measure a pleasant, profitable, and stimulating vehicle for social interaction.

3. An interesting trend is observable in the changing role of the theater in contemporary society. Where our fathers and grandfathers might have seen themselves as members of a theater audience enjoying an evening of entertainment, few if any became involved in the theater as participants finding avocational outlets. Today, however, all across the country community theaters are increasing in popularity. Encouragement is given to amateur adult theatrical groups by universities and colleges that sponsor contests in play-

writing and dramatic festivals. Specialists in all areas of the theater are sometimes made available, through extension services, to assist such groups. Many community amateur groups include specialists of their own. Audience interest, as well as production-participation interest, is often very high.

4. Following naturally from the preceding trends, we may expect an increased amount of training in communication. This seems a necessary corollary of understanding, awareness, and change.

5. As instruction increases in scope and quality, we may expect that curricula will become more uniform. Experience, experimentation, and increased specialization of workers in the field will be accompanied by the adoption of more uniform policies and programs. The studies of concepts, levels, and methods will be expanded and improved. The relationship between theory and personal proficiency will be better understood and more effectively incorporated into both school and adult programs. Philosophically sound and carefully planned programs, from the lowest through the highest levels of instruction, will begin to emerge.

6. Expansion and intensification of experimentation with both the teaching and the measurement of communication will certainly continue. Such work already in progresss may be expected to find increasing application. We have already seen the application of sophisticated experimental procedures to the analysis of communication in small groups, to statistical studies in theater aesthetics, and to the measurement of the effectiveness of persuasive appeals ranging from the most informal to such complexities as the measurement and analysis of public opinion. Many empirical observations relative to teaching procedures have been verified by experimental studies. It is unthinkable that the many other areas of great potential interest and value will remain unexplored. The utilization of experimental techniques is a necessary part of the expansion and development of the field.

7. The trend toward examination and definition of the boundaries and potentials of the discipline must continue. To the conventional and accepted sub-areas in which teaching and research have long been carried on there have been added both ramifications and refinements that require consideration. In addition to considerable advances in the area of listening, students in the field are becoming concerned with certain aspects of non-verbal communi-

cation, with the effect of social structure on oral communication, with the relationships between speaking and writing, and with the findings of anthropology, psychology, and sociology as they bear upon certain aspects of speech. The problem of ethics in communication must receive increasing attention. The place of a program of speech instruction as part of a total educational program must be more carefully explored and defined. In short, the field may be the object of greater critical attention by those in other areas as well as by students within.

8. Specialization is a characteristic of contemporary society; the field of speech will reflect this to an increasing extent. In part, this is a product of the explosion of knowledge. To some extent it may be accounted for by the opportunity that increased interest and curricular offerings in speech provide. The amount of information to be mastered is rapidly exceeding the capacity of even the most diligent scholars. No longer is it necessary for one teacher in an educational institution to handle a wide variety of different courses. Improved information-retrieval and exchange systems have made available great masses of information in almost any library, laboratory, or research center. The pace at which work in many sub-areas of the field is conducted leaves little time for interest or concern in other areas. Within the field, then, we have widely divergent interests and highly specialized training programs. This is reflected in a specialization that may be observed as early as the elementary level, where the speech therapist and the audiologist carry on unique and individual functions. It is intensified in the upper levels of teaching and research. The advantages of increased competence are not achieved without a certain price; as this trend increases, it will become increasingly important that teachers and students in the various sub-areas understand their common concern and coordinate their efforts productively. In the absence of such understanding and coordination, we can anticipate a greater variety of experiments in the patterns of administrative interrelationships within the academic community.

9. Speech education in America will flourish, struggle, or wither to the extent that our culture increases, maintains, or diminishes its present awareness of the communicative function of the citizen in a democracy. In a very real sense, the health of speech education reflects the health of our democratic tradition. This is true of the

informal education that comes from the experience of living in a culture in which speech communication is vital to human interaction and group decision-making. It is also true of the formal education supplied in the conscious attempt to prepare people to communicate with maximum effectiveness within the culture. Any meaningful measurement of either the informal or the formal dimensions of speech education, however, must be qualitative as well as quantitative.

Bibliography

Anderson, Virgil Antris, *Training the Speaking Voice,* 2nd ed. New York: Oxford University Press, 1961.

Auer, J. Jeffery, *An Introduction to Research in Speech.* New York: Harper & Row, Publishers, 1959.

Berlo, David K., *The Process of Communication.* New York: Holt, Rinehart & Winston, Inc., 1960.

Berry, Mildred Freburg and Jon Eisenson, *Speech Disorders.* New York: Appleton-Century-Crofts, Inc., 1956.

Bibliography of Speech Education, compiled by Lester Thonssen and Elizabeth Fatherson, with the assistance of Dorothea Thonssen. New York: The H. W. Wilson Co., 1939.

Bibliography of Speech Education *Supplement,* compiled by Lester Thonssen, Mary Margaret Robb, and Dorothea Thonssen. New York: The H. W. Wilson Co., 1950.

Brembeck, Winston Lamont and William Smiley Howell, *Persuasion.* Englewood Cliffs, N.J.: Prentice-Hall, Inc., 1952.

Brigance, William Norwood, ed., *A History and Criticism of American Public Address,* Volumes I and II. New York: Russell & Russell, Inc. (by arrangement with McGraw-Hill Book Company), 1960.

Bryant, Donald C. and Karl R. Wallace, *Oral Communication,* 3rd ed. New York: Appleton-Century-Crofts, Inc., 1962.

Burris-Meyer, Harold and Edward C. Cole, *Scenery for the Theatre.* Boston: Little, Brown & Co., 1941.

Cobin, Martin, *Theory and Technique of Interpretation.* Englewood Cliffs, N.J.: Prentice-Hall, Inc., 1959.

Ehninger, Douglas and Wayne Brockriede, *Decision by Debate.* New York, Toronto: Dodd, Mead & Co., 1963.

Freeley, Austin J., *Argumentation and Debate.* San Francisco: Wadsworth Publishing Company, 1961.

Gassner, John, *Producing the Play.* New York: Holt, Rinehart & Winston, Inc., 1941.

Gillette, Arnold S., *Stage Scenery: Its Construction and Rigging.* New York: Harper & Row, Publishers, 1959.

Gray, Giles Wilkeson and Claude Merton Wise, *The Bases of Speech,* 3rd ed. New York: Harper & Row, Publishers, 1959.

Head, Sydney W., *Broadcasting in America.* Boston: Houghton Mifflin Company, 1956.

Heffner, Hubert C., Samuel Selden, and Hunton D. Sellman, *Modern Theatre Practice.* New York: F. S. Crofts and Company, 1936.

Hochmuth, Marie Kathryn, ed., *A History and Criticism of American Public Address,* Volume III. New York: Longmans, Green & Co., Inc., 1955.

Hoogestraat, Wayne E. and Donald E. Sikkink, *Modern Parliamentary Practices.* Minneapolis: Burgess Publishing Co., 1963.

Irwin, John V. and Marjorie Rosenberger, *Modern Speech.* New York: Holt, Rinehart & Winston, Inc., 1961.

Johnson, Wendell, *et al., Speech Handicapped School Children,* rev. ed. New York: Harper & Row, Publishers, 1956.

Keltner, John W., *Group Discussion Processes.* New York: Longmans, Green & Co., Inc., 1957.

Lee, Charlotte I., *Oral Interpretation,* 2nd ed. Boston: Houghton Mifflin Company, 1959.

Macgowan, Kenneth and William Melnitz, *The Living Stage.* Englewood Cliffs, N.J.: Prentice-Hall, Inc., 1955.

McCandless, Stanley Russell, *A Method of Lighting the Stage,* 4th ed. New York: Theatre Arts Books, 1958.

Nichols, Ralph G. and Leonard Stevens, *Are You Listening?* New York: McGraw-Hill Book Company, Inc., 1957.

Ogilvie, Mardel, *Speech in the Elementary School.* New York: McGraw-Hill Book Company, Inc., 1954.

————, *Teaching Speech in the High School.* New York: Appleton-Century-Crofts, Inc., 1961.

Oliver, Robert T., *The Psychology of Persuasive Speech.* New York: Longmans, Green & Co., Inc., 1942.

Ommanney, Katharine Anne, *The Stage and the School,* 3rd ed. New York: McGraw-Hill Book Company, Inc., 1960.

Parker, W. Oren and Harvey K. Smith, *Scene Design and Stage Lighting.* New York: Holt, Rinehart & Winston, Inc., 1963.

Rasmussen, Carrie, *Speech Methods in the Elementary School.* New York: The Ronald Press Company, 1949.

Reid, Loren, *Teaching Speech,* 3rd ed. Columbia, Missouri: Artcraft Press, 1960.

Robinson, Karl Frederic, *Teaching Speech in the Secondary School,* 2nd ed. New York: Longmans, Green & Co., Inc., 1957.

The Role of Speech in the Elementary School. Prepared for the *Bulletin of the National Association of Secondary-School Principals,* Vol. 38, No. 199 (January, 1954).

Sattler, William M. and N. Ed Miller, *Discussion and Conference.* Englewood Cliffs, N.J.: Prentice-Hall, Inc., 1954.

Speech and Hearing Problems in the Secondary School. Prepared for the *Bulletin of the National Association of Secondary-School Principals,* Vol. 34, No. 173 (November, 1950).

A Speech Program for the Secondary School. Prepared for the *Bulletin of the National Association of Secondary-School Principals,* Vol. 38, No. 199 (January, 1954).

Syllabus for a Proposed Course in Dramatics at the High School Level, 3rd ed. Published by the American Educational Theatre Association, 1946.

Thonssen, Lester and A. Craig Baird, *Speech Criticism.* New York: The Ronald Press Company, 1948.

Van Riper, Charles, *Speech Correction: Principles and Methods,* 3rd ed. Englewood Cliffs, N.J.: Prentice-Hall, Inc., 1954.

Wallace, Karl Richards, ed., *A History of Speech Education in America.* New York: Appleton-Century-Crofts, Inc., 1954.

Ward, Winifred, *Drama with and for Children.* Washington, D.C.: U.S. Department of Health, Education, and Welfare Bulletin No. 30, 1960.

Weaver, Andrew Thomas, Gladys Louise Borchers, and Donald Kliese Smith, *Speaking and Listening.* Englewood Cliffs, N.J.: Prentice-Hall, Inc., 1956.

————, *The Teaching of Speech.* Englewood Cliffs, N.J.: Prentice-Hall, Inc., 1952.

Weaver, Andrew Thomas and Ordean Gerhard Ness, *The Fundamentals and Forms of Speech.* New York: The Odyssey Press, Inc., 1957.

PERIODICALS

American Educational Theater Association Journal. Published by the American Education Theater Association, Inc. Evanston, Ill.: Northwestern University.

The Journal of Communication. Published by the National Society for the Study of Communication. Lawrence, Kansas: Allen Press.

The Journal of Speech and Hearing Disorders. Published by the American Speech and Hearing Association. Danville, Ill.: Interstate Printers and Publishers.

National Association of Educational Broadcasters Journal. Published by the Association. Urbana, Ill.: The University of Illinois.

NUEA Discussion and Debate Manual. Published by arrangement with the Committee on Debate Materials and Interstate Cooperation, National University Extension Association, University of Oregon, Eugene, Oregon.

Quarterly Journal of Speech. Published by the Speech Association of America. Columbia, Mo.: Artcraft Press.

Speech Monographs. Published by the Speech Association of America. Columbia, Mo.: Artcraft Press.

The Speech Teacher. Published by the Speech Association of America. Columbia, Mo.: Artcraft Press.

Index